LESSON
OF
RED
DRAGON

JEANNIE HEROUX

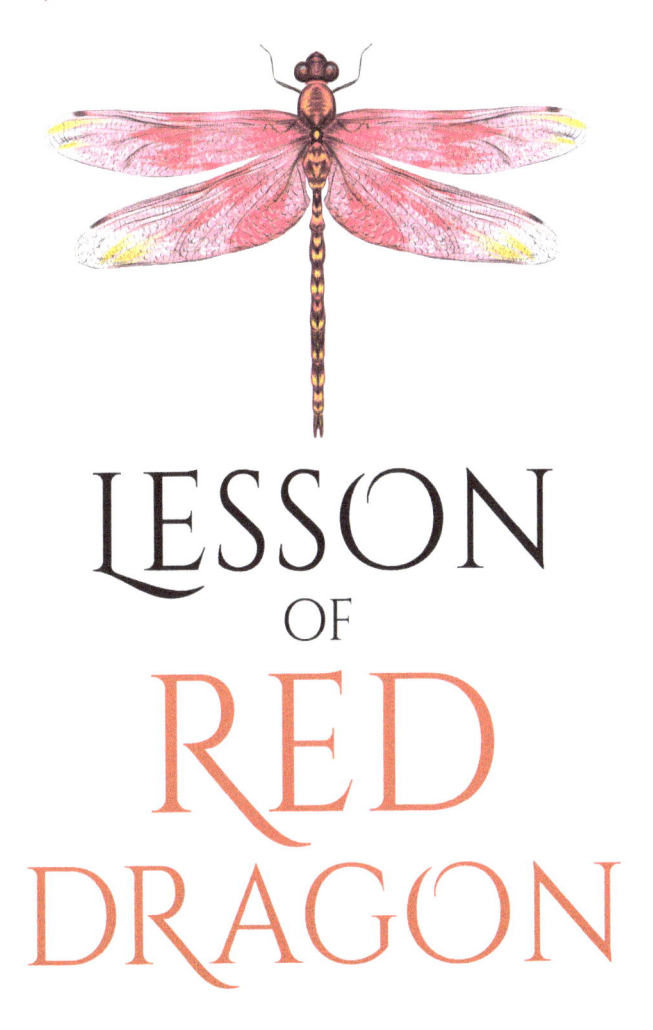

LESSON
OF
RED
DRAGON

XULON PRESS

Xulon Press
2301 Lucien Way #415
Maitland, FL 32751
407.339.4217
www.xulonpress.com

© 2022 by Jeannie Heroux

All rights reserved solely by the author. The author guarantees all contents are original and do not infringe upon the legal rights of any other person or work. No part of this book may be reproduced in any form without the permission of the author.

Due to the changing nature of the Internet, if there are any web addresses, links, or URLs included in this manuscript, these may have been altered and may no longer be accessible. The views and opinions shared in this book belong solely to the author and do not necessarily reflect those of the publisher. The publisher therefore disclaims responsibility for the views or opinions expressed within the work.

Paperback ISBN-13: 978-1-6628-5126-1
Ebook ISBN-13: 978-1-6628-5127-8

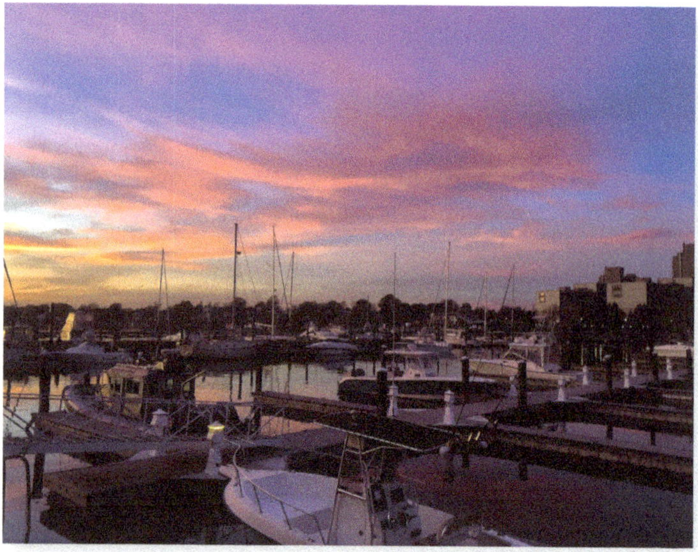

Table of Contents

Dedication/Acknowledgments. ix
Introduction xi
For My Reader / Preface xix

Chapter 1	A Foot in Two Worlds	1
Chapter 2	A Most Unusual Find.	19
Chapter 3	The Enchanting Research Begins	.25
Chapter 4	Enter Red Dragon.	38
Chapter 5	You've Got My Attention: Now What?. . . .	.51
Chapter 6	False Pride and Profound Unrest	56
Chapter 7	Lucid Dreaming	64
Chapter 8	One Wrong Choice Can Change Your Life Forever	70
Chapter 9	Andy	74
Chapter 10	Saved!.	86
Chapter 11	Return to El Bethel.	92
Chapter 12	Forty Years of Wilderness Wandering: Recovery.	.101

Chapter 13	Born Again	112
Chapter 14	Research Revisited: Dragonfly & The Red Dragon	117
Chapter 15	A Hard Path to Glory	121
Chapter 16	A Multi-Faceted Revelation	126
Chapter 17	Testing the Spirits	138
Chapter 18	The Real Ministry ~ Sober Home Living; The Affinity House	144
Chapter 19	The Long Goodbye	148
Chapter 20	Bloom Where You're Planted	152
Chapter 21	A New and Old Healthcare System: Temple of the Holy Spirit	157
Chapter 22	Andy, Revisited	167
Chapter 23	Personal Pentecost ~ The Real Magic	174
Epilogue	My Love Affair with the Holy Spirit	181
Endnotes		191

Dedication/Acknowledgments

To my daughters Christine & Catie

Introduction

God and His Creatures: What I believe

Jesus' teaching through the parables reminds us of the multitudes who saw birds, fish, sheep, oxen, trees, lilies, and fig trees in their everyday lives. They only saw them as food, or an aid to their work, or for their sacrificial system. Jesus also saw them, but He saw God revealing Himself through them, and saw them not only for their usefulness in His stories, but also because He abided in God: There was nothing that Jesus did without the authority of the Father, "Truly, truly, I say to you, the Son can do nothing of his own accord, but only what he sees the Father doing. For whatever the Father[a] does, that the Son does likewise" (John 5:19 ESV).

Jesus is the One appointed by God to be Judge of the living and the dead (Acts 10:42b) and "sits on the right hand of the Father" (Nicene Creed). Genesis 1:24-25 tells us God created the animals, from the beasts of the earth to the creeping insects. Scripture even tells us that the breath of life resides within them (Gen. 7:15). When God created animals, he declared their creation to be "good" (Gen. 1:25). At the culmination of the creation account in Genesis 1, God looked at "all he had made" and declared it all "very good" (v. 31) Spirituality, within indigenous communities and cultures is a belief that all creatures—human, animals, and plants—are interconnected. My French-Canadian background reminded me that the animal kingdom is a primary focus in the beliefs and practices of indigenous Canadians, with notable diversity in how animals are understood. They are understood as part of the human family, sources of protection, and resources of wisdom. My French-Canadian lineage includes the Métis, which is a person of mixed indigenous and Euro-American ancestry, particularly one of a group of the so-called Métis nation. I've never doubted this tribal inheritance as I've always been intensely connected to the natural world, even more so now that I understand that the natural world was made to reflect the Creator and draw us to Him.

I believe God communicates with animals. His relationship with the animals of his creation is emphasized in Job 12:7-10, "But ask the animals, and they will teach you, of the birds in the sky, and they will tell you, or speak to the earth, and it will teach you, or let the fish in the sea inform you. Which of all these does not know that the hand of the

Lord has done this? In his hand is the life of every creature and the breath of all mankind." How else do we explain the countless times we've heard stories of animals coming to human's aid, often unsolicited; or animals arriving at Noah's ark. In Genesis, God told Noah to build an ark for himself, his family, and all the animals. Nowhere does Scripture say Noah rounded up the animals. God told Noah to bring them into the ark (Gen. 6:19), which meant to simply receive them. When it was time for the flood to begin, the text says the animals "went into the ark to Noah" (Gen. 7:9). Another example of God's communication with animals, this time birds, is when the Prophet, Elijah, fled from Ahab and Jezebel (king and queen of Israel), and went to an area by the Jordan River. The Bible says God commanded ravens to bring him food while he was there, and they did (1 Kgs. 17:4-6).

I believe God works through His creation to speak to those of us who are more attuned to nature than to the voice of man, or the voice of God when He speaks in other ways. We can hear the Creator's voice in a bubbling brook, in the song of a bird, or in the wind whispering through the trees. We can see Him in the dove, the white crane, and the dragonfly.

Does the Holy Spirit call people to salvation?

The answer is an unquestionable "Yes!" Perhaps the real question is, "How???"

I believe the Holy Spirit calls certain people to salvation through what is familiar to them. "When God spoke, the way He communicated was often unique to the individual," such as the burning bush experience, specific to the shepherd, Moses—it was the only burning bush mentioned in the Bible (Blackaby).[1]

In another account of the Prophet Elijah, the Prophet was camping in a cave on Mount Sinai when God manifested Himself. Elijah saw a powerful wind, a mighty earthquake, and a fierce fire, but God wasn't in any of them. Instead, God spoke to him in a "still small voice," also translated as, "a gentle whisper" (1 Kgs. 19:9-12). God often speaks to us by the inner witness of the Holy Spirit to *our* spirit (Rom. 8:14-16).

Have you ever wondered if the Holy Spirit speaks through some living being to deliver a message? If so, what message? While the Holy Spirit usually doesn't just "appear," especially to someone who wouldn't recognize Him if He did, He has to become "believable," in order to lead someone to the Lord. Moses saw a burning bush. Moses is the only person in the Bible who had this experience.

Elijah had a wind that tore a mountain apart, then an earthquake, then a fire, but Elijah knew this wasn't God. But then, a gentle whisper, "The Lord said, 'Go out and stand on

---

[1] Blackaby, Henry & Richard with Claude King. *Experiencing God.* B&H Publishing. 2008.

the mountain in the presence of the Lord, for the Lord is about to pass by.' Then a great and powerful wind tore the mountains apart and shattered the rocks before the Lord, but the Lord was not in the wind. After the earthquake came a fire, but the Lord was not in the fire. And after the fire came a gentle whisper. When Elijah heard it, he pulled his cloak over his face and went out and stood at the mouth of the cave. Then a voice said to him, "What are you doing here, Elijah?" (1 Kings 19:11-13 NIV). God came as a gentle whisper to Elijah.

God spoke to Daniel through the Archangel Gabriel. He spoke to Jacob through his dream of a ladder. He spoke to Mary through an angel, and to Joseph through a dream. He spoke to the Magi through a star. The list goes on, but the means of communication is usually different depending on the receiver. Now I'm not putting myself in the category of the saints, but if you think about it, God probably has spoken to you using a specific form of communication that is pertinent to you alone.

I believe that as a profoundly hopeless sinner, I had to be saved. I just didn't consciously know it. So first, I had to be reached. I'm a stubborn human, so, how can the Lord touch the life of a resistant, recalcitrant teenage-minded pagan? One way is by speaking their language–through imagery, the sensual, nature, and the familiar!

John 6:63 says, "The words [Greek: rhema] that I speak to you are spirit, and they are life." The rhema Word is a specific message, usually "jumping out at us" from Scripture that the Holy Spirit murmurs to us personally. It's a Scriptural clarification for a specific time and for a particular need. It occurs when the written or spoken Word comes alive with special meaning in our situation or life. (use elsewhere?)

The following story is a personal account of my transformation, my conversion from paganism to Christianity. It originates in my encounters with a red dragonfly, who, once thought by me to be a messenger from the universe, had now caused me to speculate that this could be a messenger of The Holy Spirit. This enchanting aeronaut presented himself to me over a period of five years, and, because this is a planet for slow learners, I wasn't receiving what was being sent, at first. However, The Lord is patient. The tiny ambassador of change "showed up" for me at first as a delightful companion, and later as a beacon of joy, transcendence, and a holy messenger of miraculous awakening and ascension. After years, I finally grasped the lesson. How could I not share it?!

I believe there are many who have become engulfed in the "New Age" movement. The world of fairies, "spirits," witchcraft, oracles, goddesses, gods, and animal medicine. I was one of these many. We read the cards, interpret astrology charts, Runes, and practice what we believe to be healing modalities. Some which are, but many of which are not based on scientific principles but rather on our own perception of occult and metaphysical practices, aiming for a "new age of love and light." I held belief in the holistic form of divinity. This is the belief that divinity is infused in all of the universe, including human beings, and of course myself, with strong emphasis on the spiritual authority of the "*my self.*"

Because of my old beliefs, whomever or whatever would be sent by God to reach me would have to be someone or something I could perceive, conceive of, and believe. It would turn out to be one of His seemingly magical and miraculous creatures for whom I already had a fondness. What I used to call extraordinary coincidences became Divine appointments. What I declared to be magic I have come to know as God moments, or miracles. The latter have been a constant occurrence throughout my lifetime. They just went unrecognized and dismissed for decades until I came to know Him.

I believe wholeheartedly that this following story describes the God-led phenomenon of curious creature communication with an enchanting liaison, which later formed the spiritual foundation for a unique ministry for our Holy Lord. There is simply no other explanation. If you should find one, or are questioning some experience of your own, please feel free to contact me. redragonmagic@gmail.com

For My Reader / Preface

DO YOU EVER FEEL lost, like a perpetual stranger in this world? Do you feel like you're living a dull, mundane, ordinary, meaningless life? Maybe you're not completely aware that your life is spiritless or monotonous. Do you put one foot in front of the other, "get through" your day, completing all the necessary tasks but you still feel uninspired, as if the magic, romance, and joy of living is evading you?

Or are you financially stable, prosperous, and successful? Do you have moments of pride associated with your title and its prestige, but more and more it holds less and less meaning at the end of the day? Do you engage superficially with family or friends but still long to belong? Do you get along well with co-workers and family, but still feel isolated on-the-outside, a little hopeless, desperate even, and searching for true meaning and true love in your life? If any bit of this applies to you, chances are you don't ever admit this to anyone, not even to yourself, except in very rare, fleeting moments.

Does some aspect of you feel detached, unengaged, as if secretly waiting to be touched by the supernatural, yet also knowing you already have? You may feel a faint stirring, like a long-lost and nearly forgotten fairytale that occasionally rises to the surface of your consciousness, only to fade away again with the next momentary distraction. Every once in a while, you might muse, "there must be something more…there has to be…" In your dreams you know there is, because you harken back to timelessness, to else-others-where. Do you believe we come here from Heaven, and to Heaven we return? You're suspended in that liminal Heavenly space before birth from the womb, a state earthly words can't describe. You've caught a momentary glimpse of it, with all its colors unknown to us here, where you once had knowing, but then it vanished before it impressed itself upon your mammalian brain.

You and I, and probably all of us, have experienced this in one way or another. So, we experiment with relationships, seeking love and inclusion, or in career paths, or different geographical locations, thinking our next fulfillment is as good as our next seminar or vacation ticket. Perhaps THIS Reiki or THAT Mindfulness workshop will make me feel more purposeful. Maybe if I live in THIS town by the shore, I'll be happy. Maybe THAT person will fulfill and complete me. After a time, it seems the more modalities we try, the

For My Reader / Preface

less satisfied and empty we become. While I'd almost never admit it, that was me.

God put eternity into our hearts so that in our longing and confusion we would seek Him (Ecclesiastes 3:11). I've heard Christians speak of a "God-shaped hole" in their heart that became full to overflowing when they finally met the Lord for the first time, when they became "saved," or "born again." The believer may testify of that truly beautiful moment in time when he or she realized God was the missing piece that fit perfectly into that hole and the Holy Spirit came upon them. I'd heard and spoken to a couple of "born again" Christians and thought them to be overzealous and under-educated. I dismissed them.

I went through decades of studying astrology, Reiki, Shamanism, card reading, personal coaching, and more. In spite of studying these practices, I still felt undervalued, disconnected, weary, alienated, lost and worthless. The crazy thing is, I barely knew it! After all, to the casual observer, I had a dynamic career with prestige and prominence, with Master's and Post-Master's degrees, a vibrant social life, a large, lovely house, a Mercedes, and two beautiful daughters. What more could I possibly want?

Secretly, I wanted to belong, to feel accepted, loved, valued, connected, to be somebody, to be someone's gift. The world saw me as already having all this, but I didn't. I never did. Not ever. I say "secretly" because since I had already achieved what the "world" would call success, to admit I wanted these deeper things would be seen as weakness. I would be seen as selfish. I would be seen as foolish. And, well, I couldn't have that!

I gradually began to understand over several years that my path was becoming one of transformation, but it was not without guidance. A red dragonfly ushered me through a series of changes to a life of undreamt beauty and ultimately to God, Himself, but I had to claim myself first. I needed to truly understand, accept, then validate how I occupied my space in the world in order to allow the process to unfold. I had to own my life, love it and finally, give my life away. Think of a kid flying a kite. She doesn't stand still and wait for the kite to fly itself, but rather runs fast and trusts the wind to pick the kite up and carry it into the sky. I learned that for our life to soar, we can't stand still holding tight to how we think our dreams should happen. Instead, if we move with intention and trust The Holy Spirit to lift us, we'll get carried away!

My story will show you through the continual positive, encouraging support of the Holy Spirit, that you always belong, and you can shed your impediments and eliminate anything less than Divine. The "New Age" without God the Creator is a trick, an illusion. For me, there was no true, abiding joy in New Age. One can find the truth and open one's heart to Jesus, our Lord, and to the Holy Spirit–the Truth, the Light, the Way; and our only Savior. God opens floodgates! "Says the Lord Almighty, 'see if I will not throw open the floodgates of heaven and pour out so much blessing that there will not be room enough to store it'" (Mal. 3:10 NIV).

Remember the old Wizard of Oz movie, where it went from black & white to color? It's like suddenly living in color! You will wonder how you lived this long in colorless, passionless limbo. We don't even "see" this condition until we shed it. You see, God allows the confusion, the challenging questions, the yearning desires, all of it, so that we will earnestly pursue Him.

Once in a lifetime, something supernatural occurs. If we are open, honest with ourselves, willing to abandon our comfort zone, surrender, and humble ourselves, we can become workable and usable by God for His Kingdom. Fortunately for me, I always believed that if I wasn't living on the edge, I was taking up too much space. I've always been ready to leap empty-handed into the void, so I was well positioned to be coached by the amazing Spirit of God every step on my path to finding Jesus Christ, The Holy Spirit, and a beautiful, miraculous life in God's Kingdom–right here and now on earth!

Get ready for the ride of a lifetime.

Chapter 1

A Foot in Two Worlds

OVER THE YEARS 2012 through 2014, a being I referred to as "Snake" came to me in visions through what I refer to as lucid dreaming. Lucid dreaming feels like manipulating real life— but from within the construct of your own mind in a dream! You can travel anywhere in an instant, defy the laws of physics, change your identity, or think of something and make it happen. Sometimes these dreams develop their own script and you follow it. It may be what some people would call a "shamanic" experience. Snake was an actual character or being with a distinct personality, although he didn't always appear the same way. Sometimes he was an actual reptilian snake, other times he was almost like a cartoon version of a snake, and yet others an ethereal vision where he appeared also varied. I saw him in dreams, in real life, in my imagination, and at times I could call him up at will, feeling his essence around me. Other times, he would just show up unsolicited. I've always had a foot in this world and the other foot in another world. For encounters such as this which I will be telling you about, I could be called gifted, cursed, or just plain crazy. Whatever it's called, I can't deny what happened and it's happened a lot throughout my life.

Maybe having a foot in both worlds can be explained by this; I was born dead. My mother finally told me this story when I was well into adulthood. She told me she had been in labor for many hours. When it came time for delivery, the umbilical cord that had been wrapped around my neck 4 times, became tighter and tighter as the doctors tried to extricate me from my tiny, padded cell. The lifeline of nourishment that had kept me alive for nine months was now trying to kill me. She recounted that the doctor, after what my mom said, "seemed like forever," was heard saying to another doctor, "We've lost her." At this point my mom knew two things: Her baby was a girl, and her baby was stillborn.

She recounted that there was this long, empty silence, which was probably more like seconds, then more of nothing. There was no sound of baby cries and no sounds of childbirth as she'd known from previous births. My mom assumed the worst. She said she passed out, both from exhaustion and the horror of this apparent tragedy. She was always a bit dramatic, however, I can't say as I blamed her in this instance. She said she woke up later in the regular maternity ward and was incensed, thinking, "Why did they put me in with all these mothers with healthy, live babies?" She told me that the mothers of stillborn babies had their own area in the back of the ward, away from the busy nursery. Just then, she said that a nurse came in with a baby and said, "Here she is!" Luckily, mom said, she didn't faint a second time. Apparently, I was lost to childbirth for a few minutes until the boa-constrictor nuchal cord could be cut, and I was finally forced to officially join the world. It took many years to learn this story.

Meanwhile, I struggled with learning difficulties while growing up, among other oddities, without knowing I probably had sustained an anoxic brain injury (a traumatic brain injury, or TBI) at birth, which can cause all manners of cognitive deficits or peculiarities. While all the details are conjecture, one thing is certain; as far back as I can remember, I could see colors that others didn't see. Colors that sure weren't in my Crayola crayon box, or even in nature. I discerned beings beyond other people's perception, and on occasion I interacted with them, but always telepathically, as in no verbal discourse. I had strange but consistent words for objects that my sisters attempted to decode with little success. Everything had a color, including people, as did days of the week, and months of the year. And, I always had flying dreams that felt fantastically real, where I saw the world below me, and later in the back seat of some car, I'd recognize the terrain and know where I was. Sometimes I flew in dreams to exquisite glistening white marble palaces with long stairways up mountains; their rooms full of windows but no glass, just huge areas open to the outside. White, translucent beings drifted around me, seemingly not noticing me. In my kid's mind I was sure I was not on earth anymore.

There are too many anomalies to describe here, but I conclusively discerned that I didn't fit in or belong anywhere, as no one else told of such things. I was, well, for lack of a better word, "different" which aroused feelings of self-doubt, feelings of isolation, and of not being good enough because I was odd. But I learned that I could leave wherever I was. How? I never really quite knew. People just plain didn't see me. I don't understand it to this day. I haven't "willed" this in years because I only needed to be invisible when I was little. Pretty weird and weirder to explain, but under the right conditions I could "disappear" and venture off to other worlds, a surreal-like "journey." And journey I did! "Making" myself invisible, people would come into a room, and if I didn't want to be seen I could "make" myself unseen, and they wouldn't see me. I could go missing, only to "show up" when least expected. This proved to come in handy multiple times over my childhood, but it also just added to my list of aberrations. I kept much of these eccentricities to myself, as such tales told out of school were met with disdain or, even worse, ridicule. So,

I spent every waking moment outside, wherever I could find birds, mice, or even insects. I enjoyed their company as much as I loved climbing trees and sitting in them half the day. My best friend, Martha, and I could lounge up in a tree, listening to conversations of people passing below, and not be noticed.

Over my young years, my extra-ordinary visual perceptions faded, as my mom succeeded in beating them out of me, lest I be labeled "mental" by society, and if I brought any of my sightings to the attention of "outsiders", my mom strictly warned me, "they'll put you in the cuckoo clock and throw away the key." She was trying to protect me, as I had several family members to which this very thing had happened, and they languished in the back wards of state mental hospitals for most of their lives. There can be a fine line between gifting and just pure crazy. From my observations of the human condition, I've come to recognize certain oddities, or giftings, such as mine running in families, either as a fortuitous blessing passed along, or a vexing ancestral curse, either supported or squelched. Mine was the latter. What we do with this, or how it manifests itself, can decide whether it will be an inherited fortunate endowment, or viewed as a genetic florid psychosis.

As a kid, my French-Canadian heritage was enough to be looked upon with mild contempt, especially among those who viewed different ethnicities and cultures as decidedly "less-than" them; these "white" people, those of white Anglo-Saxon Protestant descent, people who referred to many ethnicities as "furry foreigners. Nowadays it's an archaic attitude, in fact, everyone seems to want to be "indigenous." Anyway, that we had native blood was simply a thing to be shuffled into some back file cabinet of everyone's mind. This wasn't what we refer to today as Native American lineage because we weren't American, but "furry foreigners," which in itself was barely acceptable. Having a Canadian-Indian background known as Métis was well hidden. In fact, we were sworn to secrecy, although, not by my father, who bore the heritage, but by my oldest sister, who desperately wanted to belong and be accepted by her peers. "We're Parisian French," she'd drill into us with a certain snobbish affect to her speech. Of course, nothing could be further from the truth.

My father was a stranger himself to our home due to his extensive travel for work. He was a traveling salesman, gone for weeks at a time, so in many ways I didn't really know him. It always seemed to me that he had a secret life. One thing he did reveal to me was when I was maybe 5 or 6 years old. He told me we had a Métis heritage, pronounced "matey," as in "aaarrrgghh matey," the famous Pirate salute. So, my mind ran with this. "Cool! We're Pirates," I thought to myself, and I left it at that. If I ever mentioned it to anyone, it was probably dismissed as me and my wild imagination. Later, long after I lost my father (who I never really had) when I was 27, I stumbled across information pertaining to the Métis, finally connecting that this was an "Indian tribe," not pirates. I'd had an affinity for native peoples, not necessarily Native Americans alone, but indigenous peoples everywhere, including Canada. How I wished I'd asked Dad more.

According to the Canadian Encyclopedia, Section 35 of the Constitutional Act of 1982 recognizes three Aboriginal peoples of Canada: The First Nations, Inuit, and Métis. The Métis Nation is defined as hailing from Manitoba, Saskatchewan, Alberta, parts of Ontario, British Columbia, the Northwest Territories, parts around Quebec, and the Northern United States. My father probably knew all the history, however much was lost to me as Dad was usually on the road, and he died young. From what I understood, he was a bit of an anthropologist at heart. He was a native of Trois-Rivières, a city at the confluence of the Saint-Maurice and Saint Lawrence rivers in Quebec Province.

In 1996, the Royal Commission's report stressed the importance of respecting the name that a people group chooses to give itself and the legitimacy of using the term Métis to refer to communities in Quebec, Labrador, Nova Scotia, and several other areas. Up until then, we were termed, "the other Métis;" unrecognized, and at times, hidden. Again, there had to have been an air of mystery, which would be just another "secret" that this lineage incurred.

Also in adulthood, I learned about something called "Shamanism," and I felt a vaguely familiar frequency with it, especially with its many animal spirits. Maybe there were others like me, and a Shaman's connection with nature appealed to me, as I never lost my love for the comfort of spending time outside. The idea of the Métis returned to me, and I researched this culture, feeling very strong ties. I was able to identify many "Heroux's," a very prominent surname in this tribal "nature" community, and for once I felt a sense of kinship in a world where few shared my name. The spirit of nature had often been my instructor. I never lost my awe and respect for nature as a strict, but perfect teacher who seldom grants special favor to her creatures, and less rarely gives them second chances. How humanity would be so much more aware and cautious under these same circumstances!

I informally studied Shamanism a little and learned how to use plants as medicine and aromatherapy, while also teaching others. I led groups through what I called "Nature Spirit Walks," where we would encounter birds and animals out in the woods and marshes of Cape Cod. Here I taught people the ways of the wild. I met with groups of people, led them on shamanic journeys, and held sweat lodges with a Wampanoag elder of the tribe named White Feather. We spoke of messages found in nature, the Great Spirit, and signs from our natural world.

All of this occurred well before an unusual other-worldly message would find its way to me. Was it destiny that placed me in my world and other people in theirs? Or was it The Lord that placed these worlds in us? Questions like this haunted me, although I wasn't wishing to be a seeker, as I preferred to be a finder. What follows is the story of a rare find, "a precious pearl of great price," (Matt. 13:45-46).

Working as a Nurse Practitioner at our local hospital, none of my nature excursions were ever discussed, except for my nature photography—an acceptable form of expression. Also below the radar, were my shamanic practices and my extra-sensory inclinations. Even if a colleague asked me, "How did you know that about that patient?" I'd smile, shrug my shoulders and reply, "I listen," or more commonly, "Just luck, I guess." Some peers began labeling me as an "empath," or a medical intuitive once these terms became mainstream in more recent years, so I'd leave it at that. I felt that some type of nameless spirit had always been very present in and around me.

I visited with Snake multiple times in 2012, 2013, and once in 2014, as he guided me through a process of 'shedding' old skin as he called it, "to be as if new." Snake not only appeared, but he spoke, as I just quoted him. OK, some people could be repulsed or frightened if a snake spoke to them; the whole "serpent" thing. I know many of you may have Ophidiophobia (fear of snakes), but my long-held love of nature alleviated any such concern. I also had an upsurge of actual encounters during this period of time with snakes over the course of my daily activities frolicking out in nature. What looked like a thick vine spiraling up a tree trunk would suddenly evolve into Snake, alive and slithering. Or, I'd find an actual snake out in the woods, hold him and listen to any message he might have.

Snake taught me to shed the old, like he sheds his skin, and encouraged me to just "be in your being-ness," that is, he said, telepathically, I needn't change anything or put on any "new skin," for the REAL skin underneath is already perfect, new, pure, and ready. He told me to just BE ME in my newest, perfect skin–peel away the layers, like an onion; shed anything less than Divine. He said what I have is what people hunger for, albeit the things that I hid for so long.

In some circles, snakes represent healing (Caduceus), or death, and may represent Satan (the Serpent), but most importantly here, for me, he foretold of transformation. I knew a transformation was coming for me, and what a metamorphosis I was soon to have! Snake prophesied some events that would happen over the next few years, and pretty much on schedule, most of these have come to pass as predicted.

Where did he get his knowledge? Was he demonic or did I make the things happen that he said would happen? These are the questions I would ask if I were reading this. So, let me try to answer. I believe he could have had a demonic side in that he seemed very much of the sensual world; the world of carnal urges, intimacy with nature and the creatures of the natural world. He did not, however, compel me to do anything I didn't want to do. For a time, I was a card reader. This is a person who reads cards from a deck and tells the person for whom they're reading various things about their life, their future, or just about themselves. Some people use Tarot cards or other commercially-produced cards. I actually made my own deck using photos I took of different animals, birds, and a few plants which I would "read" based on which cards the person picked from the deck. The connection here with snake reminds me of ancient Greece, when snakes were a symbol of Pythia who was the high priestess of Apollo. She used to live and prophesize inside the Delphic Oracle in Greece. Incidentally, Apollo's temple was known as The House of Snakes and later as the Delphic Oracle.[1] I had an uncanny ability to "divine" information, somewhat like the slave girl Apostle Paul encountered in Philippians.

"Once when we were going to the place of prayer, we were met by a female slave who had a spirit by which she predicted the future. She earned a great deal of money for her owners by fortune-telling. She followed Paul and the rest of us, shouting, 'These men are servants of the Most High God, who are telling you the way to be saved.' She kept this up for many days. Finally Paul became so annoyed that he turned around and said to the spirit, 'In the name of Jesus Christ I command you to come out of her!' At that moment the spirit left her" (Acts 16:16-24 NIV).

Once I became a Christian, I lost some of this ability. Did some demonic influence leave me? Well, I do know I acquired an ability to know certain things which had nothing to do with divination once I was saved, however, the Holy Spirit does help me to discern certain information, which is at times necessary for someone else's well-being or welfare.

Also, I noticed once the red dragonfly showed up, Snake disappeared completely and I haven't seen him since, nor have I seen any snakes in nature. As for information, he seemed to retrieve his knowledge from the collective reservoir of information extant in the world, or cosmos. I also think I "made" some things happen, as we are all powerful creators, maybe because we are made in the imago Dei (Gen. 1:27), or likeness of God.

There was one experience, however, that I never saw coming. While I've always perceived our earth school as a proving ground for the spiritually ill-equipped, I found myself catapulted at warp speed into a mystical, miraculous, and mysterious holy transformation. This was to be me, first meeting myself. Then the rest could follow...

Exploring Shamanism from around 2000 to 2014, I found it interesting that while I related to the concept of having spirit animals, or guides, and journeying to different levels of "worlds," I still didn't feel like I fit in here either. Although some people told me I was having "shamanic experiences," and had referred to me as "that shaman lady," whatever that meant, I still felt out of place. So, for a time I ran with it, but something wasn't right. It felt fraudulent and contrived, like I was masquerading as something I was not. although I wasn't sure why, or what I really was!

I did always feel I was destined for something more arcane and magisterial than hospital work, which was no more than my imperious self-importance looming against my fear of never belonging or not being good enough. Talk about being an ego-maniac with low self-esteem! Even though I had a prestigious title, which fulfilled me on a superficial, ego-based level, still I felt empty. I couldn't see at the time that it was a spiritual emptiness. Where I found my greatest reward was my interchanges with my patients. Listening, hearing their stories, comforting, and relating to them as a fellow human, not just as a medical provider. I did this for years, sometimes putting my whole day off schedule just to spend an hour with a patient in deep conversation, while my "true purpose" still eluded me. I couldn't see that for that moment in time, that *was* my purpose! I simply had no sense of what I was to do, or be, or where, or how, and yet I felt like I had to know. Like Yogi Berra would say, *"If you don't know where you're going, you might not get there."* Sometimes, though, I felt like some Divine Spirit was working through me and I knew just what to say to patients to help them feel better. Plus, no matter who they were, I saw myself in every single one of them, so I could always relate.

What occurred as a seeming initiation in the summer of 2015, was a lifesaver. How it happened was a game-changer. The result of these events is nothing short of a miracle. We know, however, that God's miracles are all around us every day. Still, the story I'm about to tell you is miraculous, mystical, and magical. All of us have such stories. We have only to recognize their limbic music in our hearts, and lives.

During the warm, pleasant Cape Cod summers, I'd ride my bike everywhere. I'd moved to West Yarmouth from Harwich, so I spent many days off from work exploring my new natural playground. My old area in Harwich, Bells Neck Reservoir, was replete with decades of familiarity with its woodsy ponds, marshes, deer paths, and trails. My "tribe" has always been "we who fly," primarily birds: The Bird Tribe. I've had a love of and affinity for birds since I can remember. I'd play with our parakeets for hours as a 3-year-old. As a kid, I had several birds as pets, and at night I had vivid dreams of flying. I flew over buildings, roads, towns, and cities only to eventually go there and know exactly where I was because I'd been there before. Like some spirit in the night, I saw places before ever physically going.

In adulthood, I particularly loved the graceful, solitary, and patient Great Blue Heron. I related to his demeanor as a loner. I also had a liking for fairies and angels, as did one of my sisters, Nancy, which intensified for her just months before she died. They were all messengers and flyers. My new area of cranberry bogs, ponds, and woods still seemed to have the same plant life, woodland creatures, and waterfowl. Of course, my new locale was only two towns away from my old one.

Being a nurse practitioner at the local hospital ER, I worked a lot, although I never really felt like I belonged there. Being a lover of nature, I longingly looked out any window that I might chance to hurry past while pounding the concrete halls, and since I was cooped up inside all throughout my work shift, I was compelled to escape to the outdoors for hours during my time off. Again, I lived with a foot in two worlds. I'd blast out of the hospital doors after work like a caged thing just finding freedom, gasping in fresh air and sun. Later, I'd take photos of all that caught my interest. If I didn't find something amazing during the day, it wasn't much of a day. Spoiler alert: There's always something amazing!

One of my heart's desires was, and still is, to capture nature through photographs to share with people who are unable, or perhaps unwilling to trudge through the brush, blazing trails where no one goes, to enjoy these wonders themselves. People often thank me for "delivering nature's best," as their "Nature Spirit Guide," a name I earned for this joyful task.

You see, nature taught me almost everything I knew about life, about death, about persisting despite a plethora of challenges. Out here, the calm greenness abounds after a rainfall. All is quiet, but for the sounds of nature's native tongue. Even though the swan may have lost her mate to the coyote last night, or Mamma Duck lost 4 babies to the fox, they still swim, fly, eat, and live. Nature is strict—a tough teacher who rarely gives second chances.

But still, the Heron fishes, Osprey dive for dinner, and crows call among the trees while others answer. The honeybee gathers, the squirrel collects, trees sway in the breeze, and sweet Pepperbush exudes an alluring aroma.

The orchestral tapestry of drama plays out in nature among the inhabitants, far from the busyness of the modern world, but the sounds have no stridency. Here in this marsh is just the music of the vast Deep. The Creators' silence, the language of The All That Is.

A woodpecker taps on the tree behind me as if in code. The bullfrog's robust chorus blends in with the chickadee's diverse repertoire. This is Sanctuary. This IS peace.

Whatever sadness, worry, shame, guilt, grief, or anger that might plague us; it is dissolved here. It is minutiae. It holds no high importance anymore. The glory and greatness of creation diminishes to trivia what once seemed an abysmal tunnel of darkness.

Rabbit still freezes at the sound of footsteps. Fish still jump to try to catch the elusive dragonfly. Mushrooms still pop through loose earth and seeds still take purchase upon fertile soil.

And I still watch, listen, feel, inhale, and exhale the miraculous breaths of Life. I am forgetting about anything that is less than Divine while receiving subtle messages from my co-conspirators out here, knowing that nature is the closest connection to God that we can experience here on earth.

This is why I am a Nature Spirit Guide, that is, a guide to the Spirit of God through the lens of nature: A nature photographer. My life is a spirit walk in nature and I'm always thrilled to bring people along, however they wish to be a part, even if simply delivering nature in photographs.

We "see," and I mean truly see—by waking up! We know our life experientially and embrace it with passion, love, and purpose.

There's no rush in nature. Events unfold in their own time—God's time. He has no calendar. When we let go of "needing" answers, then messages meant just for us appear. When we are free of our desire to control, events occur in synchronized perfection. When we surrender to vulnerability, we are empowered. But where does nature come from? I had spent my life pondering such things. If nature is not the source of itself, then what or who is? This and more would be answered in a most mysteriously delightful way.

Chapter 2

A Most Unusual Find

ONE JULY DAY, RIDING my bike home from my new favorite cranberry bog, I saw something out of the corner of my eye on the sidewalk as I rode past. Upon stopping and backing up, what I saw on close inspection was thrilling, yet poignant. I bent down to inspect a 3-inch long red dragonfly, perfect, yet dead, lying on the cement. I picked him up and observed his wings. The glistening gold-copper filament maintained its structural integrity and his jewel-red body was completely intact. Perhaps he flew into the windshield of an oncoming car and was propelled to the sidewalk. I gently held him in my hand as I got back on my bike and rode home. I left him out in the air for a while in case he was only stunned and came to, though I was pretty sure this wouldn't happen. I placed him in a container, feeling sad for this loss, and awed at the glory of this huge red dragonfly. I had never seen such a creature in all my outdoor adventures.

Several days later, I was out in the marshy bog sitting on a large, fallen tree overlooking the shallow water of a small inlet, which feeds into a pond to the west of the bog. Suddenly, I felt someone very close by. I felt watched. I'm pretty vigilant out alone in the woods, so I'm usually aware of someone before they're aware of me, but not this time. Looking down to my left, I saw a little red dragonfly, as if a miniature version of the one I'd found days before. He shifted his small 1-inch-long body until he was actually facing me. I welcomed him and took several pictures, all for which he remained eerily still, perched about six inches away. We sat there like that for thirty minutes or so, and then I decided to move on. I said goodbye to him and thanked him for sitting with me.

I peddled aways, came to another favorite spot, and sat down to take in the scenery. Once again, feeling a presence I looked to my side and spotted a small red dragonfly. He oriented himself to face me, and we sat in silent space like this for about fifteen minutes. There was a certain peace, yet excitement around this beautiful new friend. Once again, I said goodbye to him, thanked him for sitting with me and for allowing me to photograph him.

My next day out around the bogs, I encountered the red dragonfly again. This time I saw him fly toward me and land in a Sweet Pepperbush with its distinct lush aroma wafting from fresh blooms. The red dragonfly landed before me, with a side-view, but quickly reoriented himself until he was looking at me head-on. I had a chance to study him, take a few pictures, and chat. I told him how happy I was to see him again and complimented him on his ruby-red gemlike body, with golden-copper glistening wings, so delicate. He sat there, head moving back and forth in between long gazes toward me. His tiny mouth seemingly moving quickly, as if whispering back in conversation, his secrets to me – and I, in response, oh spirit, wind-traveler, utter tales of your wondrous world to me.

We sat for some time before I thanked him and said farewell. I invited him to come with me and stopping at my next destination, there was a red dragonfly awaiting my arrival. Several other red dragonflies arrived, flew around, landed, left, and landed again. One or two landed on my shoulder and knee, coming and going. I could not ever recall the kiss of a dragonfly until that day. In fact, I'd had no commerce with them at all in all my years outdoors.

By the third or fourth day of visiting with the red dragonfly, I began addressing him as Little Dragon or Red Dragon, or more often just "Red." He'd show up, land, and orient his position, while I excitedly greeted him, "Hi Red!" My solar plexus area that feels all bubbly and tingly whenever I believe a spirit touches me would be activated, so when I greeted him, telling him how happy I was to see him, my body resounded with my words of appreciation and joy. I felt a buoyancy in his company. We'd sit for thirty minutes, sometimes more, until I wanted to move on. He politely never left first.

My mother had died in February of this same year, and I wondered if Red was her way of getting my attention. It seemed plausible at first, although my mom had no interest in dragonflies or nature for that matter, staying indoors most of her life. Still, as time went on I kept this in mind. There was much more yet to be revealed. I also recalled Snake's message of shedding the old, and I knew this tiny change-agent was a messenger for a similar phenomenon. Snake was no longer at the forefront of my awakened self, having receded into the background of memory.

Again, "conversation" with Red was telepathic–no spoken words. During my pond-side "chats" with the little red dragonfly, the aromas of nature; flowers, plants, trees, bogs, marshes, ponds, oceans, and the sensory means of nature's language, filled my space. Our olfactory system's nerves connect directly to brain structures of the limbic system so the connection between our sense of smell and emotions is unlike that of the other senses. It is the limbic area, this ancient brain's region, that our emotions, memories, passions, fears, and longings are stored, so it is no wonder that nature's aromas create the "limbic music"[2] of our heart's and soul's desires. Steeped in this olfactory euphoria of fragrance, a little red dragonfly was messaging me heart-to-heart, in Nature's native tongue, from what seemed like the core of his collective spirit as a species, to mine.

I realized I had to pay attention. I'd write down the perceived messages from my new friend. The chemical romance between floral pungency and our feelings stir the melody of limbic memories like an orchestral tapestry of the soul; lavender, lilac, honeysuckle, awakening a sense of wonder and of a Creator who surely made everything. I felt like I was remembering lifetimes ago, yet all was in this lifetime, in this moment, right in this 'now.' Ah, such a wonder!

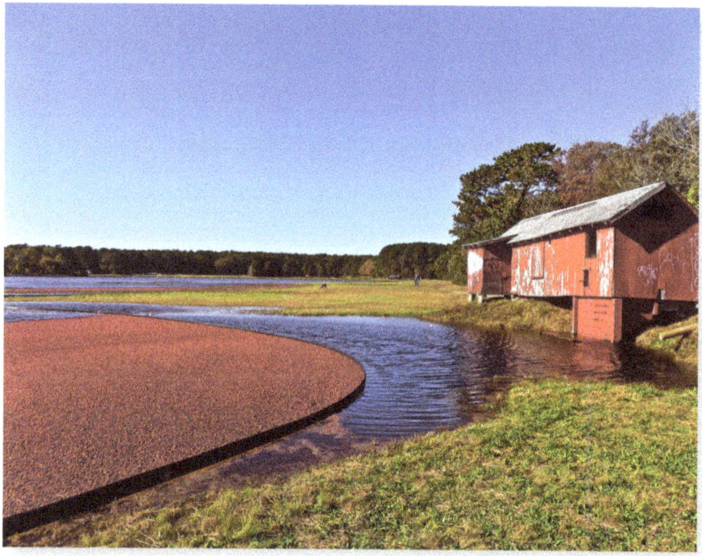

Chapter 3

The Enchanting Research Begins

LIKE ALL INVETERATE SCIENTISTS, I performed research on dragonflies; gathering data and learning everything I could from whatever practical information was available for the red dragonfly, commonly called an Autumn Meadowhawk, or by its genus-species name, Odonate, sympetrum vicinum.

My first encounter with him was in mid-July and lasted through late Fall. He appeared yearly mid-July. There is a Japanese Haiku:

> *"That the autumn season has begun is decided by the appearance of the red dragonfly."*

The Chinese calendar is slightly ahead of ours.[3] The red dragonfly is the only species of insect who stays beyond what climate one would think would be conducive to and compatible with insect life. The last vestiges of Fall are swept out with the shifting sands of winter. The beach is devoid of life, except for the seagulls' lonely cries. Ponds are lifeless and still, as if frozen, no gliding ducks, no jumping fish. But a little red dragonfly sits, filigree wings blowing in a chilling, biting breeze, awaiting certain death, well into December.

I found that dragonflies have inhabited our planet for nearly 300 million years. Dragonflies are water creatures until they develop wings and become airborne. They remain near water for mating and laying their eggs at the water line, usually with their mate still attached. The eggs hatch, and the immature dragonflies remain underwater for most of their lives, up to 4 years. When they emerge with wings to fly, this part of their life is relatively short, only around 2 months. They have 360-degree vision, seeing in all directions, including behind them, as they fly forward. The psychological beauty of this remarkable ability didn't escape me. Imagine flying with our past behind us in our sight, but always moving away from it and propelling forward while maintaining presence. They spend their time soaring, like tiny stunt-flyers, consuming large quantities of insects, especially mosquitoes, mating, and laying eggs.[4]

And apparently, sitting with me.

Consider this spiritual analysis: A master of flight, he could dart hither and yon, and appear as if from nowhere, like an angel. He was male, as evidenced by his jewel-red color. The females are a dusty brown. Red is the color associated with the Pentecost. Red is the color of the shed Blood of Christ. Red is also associated with Christmas, the birth of Christ. Red is the color of the figurative heart of Love. Dragonflies move about like spirits. The dragonfly, I found, is also a symbol of growth and development. He is strongest when he stays close to his source of strength, the sunlight. He absorbs warmth from the sun. It is like he reflects it through his wings to enlighten the world. From a Godly perspective, as we absorb God's light, the Holy Spirit teaches, guides, and shines through us so others are drawn to Him. What I found from a spiritual standpoint fascinated me. I learned that the dragonfly can serve to remind us that we too can reflect the light of Christ in a darkened world.[5]

This intrigued me, as I had not paid much attention to religion, having had only a vague introduction to God in my youth, and no real notion of Jesus, except for during the holidays of Christmas and Easter. Even though I raised my children in the Catholic church, I still didn't really ever "get it." Yet I felt a quickening; something awakening.

Finally, I considered the impeccable anatomy of the dragonfly. Science often turns to nature to replicate a perfect design, and in this case it has observed and attempted copying the dragonfly for flight. Trying to duplicate the dragonfly science payload, NASA is presently considering the dragonfly concept, among many other proposals for missions to Venus, Titan, Enceladus, comets, and other targets.[6]

If scores of intelligent scientists had to expend vast amounts of time, energy, intention, deliberation, knowledge, and thought, in order to discover the secrets of the efficient motions of the dragonfly, what must have been required to actually create that dragonfly in the first place? Mindless, non-intelligent, unconscious, non-purposeful "evolutionary" forces? I think not. The dragonfly is a testament to the Creator.

Time and chance do not and cannot account for the amazing design found in marvels like the dragonfly. The only logical, plausible explanation I could find is that dragonflies were designed by a Creator. I began thinking of Red Dragonfly as a miraculous being, a spirit descended to Earth, as if by magic. Incidentally, the word 'magic' comes from an ancient Iranian word, borrowed into Greek that gave us the name "Magi" which was given to the 3 Wise Men in Matthew 2:11.[7]

I've heard from the Christian community that one must be cautious with magic as it may be associated with Lucifer. Historically, "Beings of Light" have often been quite to the contrary. I wondered if I was being tricked. Later in my musings, I considered he really might be one of God's messengers, testifying to His wisdom. As the years passed, the notion of God's influence was becoming more plausible. It occurred to me that with so precious little time above water as a flying being, why would the red dragonfly spend so much time sitting with a human? It had already become obvious to me that "Red" was spending a great deal of time with me every day. Of course, there were many red dragonflies, not just one, but why—as a species—were they showing up to sit with me? Prior to now, I'd never even seen a *red* dragonfly.

Clearly these were not just social visits. Red dragonfly had aroused my attention, seemed to have a message for me, and apparently had committed to staying close until I understood what it was. I began to contemplate what that directive might be. I never actually thought to directly ask him, "Who are you?" It seemed impolite.

This is a creature who is an extremely impressive aeronaut. Like hummingbirds, they fly erratically, covering multiple planes and dimensions instantaneously in flight, adapting to whatever they encounter. Unlike hummingbirds, however, sometimes, they are simply suspended in the air, wings still, letting the breeze carry them off a distance, just gliding as the wind takes them, and they can even do all of this while mating! Flexibility and adaptability are hallmarks of this incredibly talented flyer.

Dragonflies also are creatures of water and air with "a foot in both worlds" beginning in one element; water, and ending in another; air, but always staying close to water. Maybe this is partly why I so related to them. They don't lose sight of the water element once transforming into a different version of themselves and becoming of the air element. Still, they can't ever return to their old form or life below the surface once they transcend it and fly into their airy realm. They can never go "home" again.

This isn't a bad thing. Consider this story of the waterbug to dragon fly transformation:

"Down below the surface of a quiet pond lived a little colony of waterbugs. They were a happy colony, living far away from the sun. For many months they were very busy, scurrying over the soft mud on the bottom of the pond. They did not notice that every once in a while one of their colony seemed to lose interest in going about with its friends. Clinging to the stem of a pond lily, it gradually moved out of sight and was seen no more….

Finally, one of the waterbugs, a leader in the colony, gathered its friends together. "I have an idea," he said, "the next one of us who climbs up the lily stalk must promise to come back and tell us where he or she went and why."

One spring day, not long after, the very waterbug who had suggested the plan found himself climbing up the lily stalk. Up, up, up he went. Before he knew what was happening, he had broken through the surface of the water, and had fallen onto the broad, green lily pad above. When he awoke, he looked about with surprise. He couldn't believe what he saw. A startling change had come to his old body. His movement revealed four silver wings and a long tail....

The dragonfly remembered the promise he had made when he had been a waterbug: "The next one of us who climbs up the lily stalk will come back and tell where and she went and why."

Without thinking, the dragonfly started down. Suddenly he hit the surface of the water and bounced away. Now that he was a dragonfly he could no longer go into the water.

"I can't return!" he said in dismay. "At least I tried, but I cannot keep my promise. Even if I could go back, not one of the waterbugs would know me in my new body. I guess I will just have to wait until they become dragonflies too. Then they'll understand what happened to me, and where I went."

And the dragonfly winged off happily into its wonderful new world of sun and air."[8]

Just like the waterbug transforms into a dragonfly and cannot return to its old self, I found myself transforming, no longer able or wanting to return to my old self. But again, this isn't a bad thing.

Finally, in my analysis, as noted before, the red dragonfly is jewel-ruby-red; the color of passion, love, creativity, Pentecost, and the red fire of the Heart. Putting it all together, I had adaptability, transformation, dual elements, Divine

Spirit, magic, creativity, passion, and love. On a global scale, dragonfly's powerful and unique metamorphosis could be a metaphorical message for the transformation humanity is now undergoing. For some of us, the time has come to go inward and embark on the intrinsic journey of consciousness expansion, emerging from the heavier dimensions to the less dense. My belief is that in the atmospheric realms (like Paul speaks of 1st, 2nd and 3rd heavens) as we progress in our Christ-consciousness, we actually become "lighter" for lack of a better description, moving toward our heavenly home even while we are "here" physically on earth we can become closer. I do it through fasting & prayer and meditation. Humanity is ascending, with some of us going willingly, while others choose to remain enslaved in drama and toxicity. This is an evolution of the *self*. But it is an expansion of the self that merges eventually with the Christ; not completely here on earth, but the convergence is a process, like that of sanctification.

On a personal scale, he heralded in my own consciousness—a conversion, from one who hid my God-given gifts to one who would eventually recognize and pursue Christ, begging for the salvation that was already mine, exposing the true me, although I didn't yet have an inkling of this. My own unrecognized brokenness would find healing as I ascended from the depths of an old paradigm up to the lighter, more sublime realms. Things such as selfishness, pride, and other sins carry a certain gravity with them, that is, they weigh us down. What many refer to as "baggage" from their past is usually things of this sort. But as we grow spiritually, any iniquities, transgressions, and enmities that we lug along with us through life begin to fall away; it is a "shedding" process. But first, I would have to acknowledge that I needed fixing. As I later found, this is sometimes how God works. He uses unusual or peculiar people, creatures, and instances to speak to us.

All of us who seek to glorify God can only do so in our own unique way, to reach our own specific tribe or community, and bring them along in our transformation. Our own distinct means in spreading the Word of God first demands finding it, then it would require a distinct guide, a Spirit Guide, who could burst through my reticence to entertain any sense of holiness. Like I said, I was stubborn! Looking back, I wasn't fighting Satan most of my life, we got along just fine. I was fighting God!

Learning of his history, symbolism, and meaning still left questions regarding what Red Dragon meant for *me*. And, why me? I felt like I was being called to be a portal through which love, passion, and God's blessings flow out into the world. Waves of liquid love. Red dragonfly was (and still is) a tangible spirit: I believe all creatures have a spirit. When they die they look deflated, just like humans do; their spirit leaves their body. If you've ever had a pet die, you know they no longer look like their vital self as when their spirit was in them.

Red and I held communion each summer and fall for five years. There have been changes, however. While I still catch glimpses of Red, he no longer stops and sits for hours and for days with me. I am not hearing his succinct messages as clearly anymore. If he does fly by, once in a while he stops and lands by me for a couple of minutes, but then he's off again into the gleaming summer light. Still, I sense that Red continues to bring messages to our world today, as many people still need to receive them. He is bringing a collective message to us now that humanity must heal the wounds of separation between the Holy Spirit within and our outer expression (the flesh), returning to living wholly, and holy, from our brokenness in the sacred heart of Jesus.

I felt he also brought a warning, as we—our global society—continue to disregard our Earth and our Heavenly Father. Living for ourselves, selfishly, and dismissing one another as violence and chaos reign. We must take heed, giving up our own selves once we have found ourselves. I know it sounds contradictory, but for me anyway, I spent such a long time building myself up, gaining self-esteem, working on being proud of my accomplishments, but as I grew in Christ, the Holy Spirit prompted me to relinquish my pride, my accomplishments, and not esteem myself. What took me thirty years to build up, I'd need to tear down; strongholds that kept me separated from God. We can't give away what we don't have. I had to first grasp this life with all its self-importance, because I came to believe we cannot keep our lives but must give them away; first to Christ, then in service to one another. You see, in the world we are taught the way of upward mobility. In Christ, it's just the opposite—downward mobility, "For those who exalt themselves will be humbled, and those who humble themselves will be exalted." (Matt. 23:12 NIV).

At this point, I still hadn't cracked a Bible, and if I did, I quickly put it down, not understanding it at all. If I really tried to decipher it, I'd be setting my feet where the sand was untrodden. I knew nothing of Eschatology, of end times, of the Book of Revelation. Still, in retrospect, my ponderings weren't terribly far from some Biblical concepts. During one of our last visits, Snake reminded me, "That skin is getting looser." I clearly identified with the shedding of the old, like as Apostle Paul would say, putting off the old self, "You were taught, with regard to your former way of life, to put off your old self, which is being corrupted by its deceitful desires" (Eph. 4:22 NIV).

I already knew I love people. I couldn't do hospital work if I didn't. But I also had been developing a stronger sense of loving unconditionally, and in a less restrictive setting. The further our love extends, the bigger our heart grows, rippling out from us in concentric circles. Wisdom understands that we all need space. Love combined with space is, essentially, the impetus for letting go of our earthly attachments, and thus our suffering. I would come to learn that "Anyone who does not love does not know God, because God is love" (1 John 4:8).

Indeed, I felt myself feeling more distanced from my job, just putting in my time. I could hardly wait to leave work so I could be "out there" with nature, in my favorite exquisite surroundings. I could barely contain myself until I got there and could see Red. I knew a transformation was eminent and that I was teetering on the precipice, more than I understood right then. But I wasn't at all clear on how it would unfold. I felt that the process of "letting go" was incorporated into my shedding of my old self.

Chapter 4

Enter Red Dragon

SOME FRIENDS AND FAMILY have described me as a risk-taker, even quixotic at times regarding my dreams and goals, with no conquest too great. Boldness in the face of change takes courage, and I, being no stranger to the outrageous, was definitely up for the challenge. I was just in the dark as to precisely how that would look. Then a turning point came.

Once, I was in the cranberry bog looking at a tree directly in front of me, and I realized there were three red dragonflies in triangle formation. There was one on a branch to my right, one on a branch to my left, and one directly above, half-way between the other two. All three were oriented to be looking directly at me.

"The Holy Trinity!" I actually blurted out loud! I hadn't thought of the Holy Trinity in decades, from the scant Christian knowledge that I had sequestered away from childhood. All three viewed me face-to-face. Chills and joyful tears wracked my body, heart, and soul. "What IS this!?!? Why are you guys here? Is this a sign of the real, "Holy Trinity?" I was almost delirious with awe. What was the meaning of this message? And why? What did it have to do with me and what was I to do with it? Something shifted in me after that experience. But what? As I look back now, this was the heralding in for conversion, I just couldn't recognize it yet. I was blind, but now I see.

As the days passed, I listened for more details of red dragonfly's message. The Holy Trinity pervaded much of my imagination. Visions, metaphors, language heretofore unknown to me except for in dreams, filled my mind, heart, and spirit. The message of hope, faith, and knowledge that there was/is a higher calling and power elevated my entire being to a new level of ascension, as I felt myself becoming lighter, and my mind more spacious. The old "higher power" of A.A. was ratcheted up a couple octaves. "That we worship one God in trinity and the trinity in unity, neither blending their persons nor dividing their essence. For the person of the Father is a distinct person, the person of the Son is another, and that of the Holy Spirit still another. But the divinity of the Father, Son, and Holy Spirit is one, their glory equal, their majesty coeternal."[9]

In October 2015, I had 4 days off and I spent them on an internal vision quest. This wasn't about sleep deprivation, isolation, fasting, or braving elements in the woods, as are the vision quests in Native American culture. This was about internal intention. Intention is the force that sets in motion all manner of action, of change, because intention is not so much a desire but our exercising of our will. Each choice we make is a choice of intention. I planned on going inward and seeking myself, my own spirit, to fully understand my intentions in "getting definite with the Infinite" regarding my new path, transformation, and perhaps my career. What I hadn't considered was that the "infinite God" wasn't just within me, but all around me. He is omnipresent.

"The God who made the world and everything in it, being Lord of heaven and earth, does not live in temples made by man, nor is he served by human hands, as though he needed anything, since he himself gives to all mankind life and breath and everything. And he made from one man every nation of mankind to live on all the face of the earth, having determined allotted periods and the boundaries of their dwelling place, that they should seek God, and perhaps feel their way toward him and find him. Yet he is actually not far from each one of us, for 'In him we live and move and have our being,' as even some of your own poets have said, 'For we are indeed his offspring'"(Acts 24-28 ESV).

God has His own plans. I hoped to use this time to speculate over the true lesson of this red dragonfly, which I did, spending hours outdoors daily with my friend. Red sat with me in his characteristic fashion all day, every day, for these 4 days while I had no human contact or social media interaction whatsoever. This is what I discovered and uncovered:

Red dragonfly seems well aware that as a species, they are as endangered as we are. As humanity has become more separate from nature AND from our spiritual source, we have lost our '*roots*'. Many people disregard our planet, spend less time outdoors and less time in community, eerily disconnected from each other despite the supposed "connectivity" offered by the internet and the World Wide Web. We've lost knowledge of the miracle of life, in fact, we disregard it, as evidenced by the deluge of terminated pregnancies in our world. In fact, I was guilty of this myself, and this kept me feeling unworthy of any God for the first half of my life. It wasn't until I realized it's under the blood; Christ died for murderers too. I had to see it this way. Apostle Paul murdered Christians, yet he was covered with the blood of Christ. Anyone reading this who feels doomed or damned for things you've done in your past, repent! And be saved. God doesn't love the sin, but He loves us. THIS is a miracle!

The sun rises every day, THIS is a miracle! That we draw in breath every day, THIS is a miracle! That our hearts dutifully go on beating. THIS is a miracle. A sperm and an egg unite and against many odds, they create a human. THIS is a miracle. And the miracle of unconditional love; do we really even know what this is? At one point, Red hinted at part of my purpose as being a "light-worker," although I didn't even know what that term was or what it meant, but it sounded "New Agey." He may have meant something different, but this is the term that I interpreted. It was something good, a higher vision it seemed; an invocation of non-physical dimensions, and it made my hospital work make more sense, bringing light to a dark place.

Later, I would learn of this in the Olivet Discourse: "You are the salt of the earth. But if the salt loses its saltiness, how can it be made salty again? It is no longer good for anything, except to be thrown out and trampled underfoot. You are the light of the world. A town built on a hill cannot be hidden. Neither do people light a lamp and put it under a bowl. Instead, they put it on its stand and it gives light to everyone in the house. In the same way, let your light shine before others, that they may see your good deeds and glorify your Father in heaven" (Matt. 5:13-16).

Once, when sharing my growing dismay at my 50-hour/week hospital job, a friend reminded me, "Hospitals need light workers too!" She used that term and I understood what she was saying. Maybe that's why I understood Red, whether he meant it in this context or not; Salt and light.

As a member of my social circle, my self-appointed purpose, I told myself, had been to reach out to others, stretch their perceptions, encourage them to go beyond their comfort zone, dare them to explore and go beyond their self-imposed limits. It was also to share insights, spread joy, speak the language of love and of spirit with all who travel this frequency of a higher ground, and infuse my surroundings with nature and its photography. But all this sort of talk had become part of the "New Age" lexicon to which I'd become accustomed, having pretty much lost the little superficial religious values I gleaned from youth.

I never really understood religion or church as a kid. We learned there was a God, but He was so remote, unreal, and often so angry! Gosh! The wrath! Still, it seems the biggest mistake we ever made as a culture was to put God up in the sky somewhere, removing Him from the rivers, golden fields, and blades of dew-covered grasses. We memorized a couple of lifeless, loveless prayers which were recited by rote, while we sat stiff in our rigid pews, with little awareness of our prayer's meaning. Perhaps prayer was once a dance, an arabesque and pirouette, or maybe an ecstatic, inspired, swinging, swaying cha-cha or samba. If so, we never knew.

Jesus was a guy hanging on a cross who we heard about only around Easter and Christmas. He wasn't someone we could even dream of feeling close to, much less walk with or have a relationship with. We didn't learn of the full depth or breadth of His suffering, His agony, the messiness of His excruciating death, His humanness. No, in my limited experience, churches had sterilized Christianity, enshrouding the intimacy of the Jesus relationship with dogma and inaccessibility; this Man/God who robbed me of being a stranger over 2000 years ago had been made unavailable under the guise of "religion."

My family of origin never opened a Bible. Looking back, I find this sad, as the Bible is really a magnificent, long and enduring love-letter to us from God. Scripture was actually alien to me, so I didn't entertain it, but rather sought out nature as my "God." As time went on, the seemingly contrived and often spurious ideology of the New Age agenda was slowly corroding, becoming more hollow and hypocritical. I really didn't know where, how, or if I fit in anywhere anymore.

So again, I felt like I didn't belong anywhere. Still, I believed there had to be a place for me. It was clearly time to finally understand and claim my space here on this earth plane. But as what? And how? And where? As who?

While my work in allopathic medicine, i.e., Western or modern medicine like we see in hospitals today, had its usefulness, I thought perhaps a new role would be an amalgam of all my previous knowledge and "fieldwork" of Tai Chi/Qigong, aromatherapy, herbal medicine, and medical training, along with my expanded experiences acquired through my immersion in nature and now, this synchronistic acquaintance with a red dragonfly, which I could amass, bringing new blessings to the world. I wasn't sure how this would occur. What I did know, or at least I thought I knew, was that I was gradually separating from the mainstream medical community with its reliance on Big Pharma and other chemical cures, and was seeking to offer people a different kind of healing. This, of course, would take a different turn than I had ever imagined it could have back then.

I'd been studying and seeking to find my true purpose while taking courses to be a personal coach. I liked this idea. I was working on the paradigm of magic–that enchanting and mysterious, other-worldly force, with the outline being that my essence was magic. My purpose was to create magic in people's lives. My vision was to create magical blessings in the world, creating heaven on earth. I would coach people to find their own personal magic, their own blessings, just as red dragonfly was doing with me, when he would 'show up' for me and touch the core of my being. Then, in a ripple effect, I, in turn, would reach out and touch others, and then they would reach out, touching others—a glorious wizard's wand of mystical, magical, catalytic change.

Magic was clearly the theme. It was not meant in a classic sense as the apparent influence on the course of events by using supernatural forces, like a spell or some weird voodoo. It was a more casual meaning, more like something wonderful and exciting, as in "magic moments," or a "magical sunset." Of course, we can say that any act or vision of beauty holds a supernatural aspect, for we know we could never replicate it; it is beyond our means. Thus, we view these occurrences as heavenly, divine, and consider them blessings. Even when I take photos of some exquisite natural phenomenon, it never comes out as vivid or as stunning in a pictorial depiction on paper as when viewed in person.

Once I became a true Christian, I would come to question the meaning of "magic," as it applies to Lucifer. Lucifer is that oft-appearing 'being of light,' or, "Light-Bringer," who, with his temptations, can provide us the opportunity to see and learn in the form of temptation, incurring a negative result if we would act on it, creating sin. And make no mistake, Lucifer won't appear like a pinnacle of malfeasance; some horrific, repulsive creep like we'd expect, but rather, he shows up as the most beautiful, seductive, desirable version of something or someone we've always dreamed of having. Lucifer also has the uncanny ability to prey on your innermost hunger while always inserting a kernel of truth to whatever he's communicating, so if we're not vigilant, he is almost believable. He'll tell us, "try just a little," or, even worse, "entertaining it in your mind isn't hurting anyone."

I came to discover over time that walking that delicate line between temptation and acting upon it is a precarious, slick, and slimy slope, reminding me that God, like nature, is a very just and stringent teacher. God is holy, and whatever isn't can't exist with Him. Our heart isn't like a timeshare. We can't rent it out to Satan for 6 months and to God the other 6 months. God can't abide. It's all God or no God.

For the time being, however, for me, magic had no negative connotations, as not being a Christian, I was not fully awake to all the significance and ramifications. After all, I'm the one since early childhood who had endless seemingly "magical" adventures in the animated spaces of my imagination, or perhaps dreams. Some were so real, I just can't even begin to describe them, and it always had been this way.

Frequently, I found that magic was manifested in nature. Taking people on Nature Spirit Walks, creating "Nature Spirit Photography," felt like "home" to me. The walks were silent, meditative strolls through Bell's Neck Reservoir, just being in nature, seeing wildlife, and connecting with whatever energies or animals attracted individual people or the group. The photos were wildlife action shots, stills, or colorful, dramatic vistas of the ocean, marshes, woods, and ponds. I enjoyed capturing the ambiance and soul of the outdoors and sharing this as a Nature Spirit Guide and photographer. Yet, I knew this wasn't the endgame for me. Being a coach was a stepping stone but it was not entirely ringing true for me either. When you have a gift, but you don't yet know the Giver, it is hard to know just exactly how to use that gift correctly.

Here is what I understood: Red had to show up for me in a form that I would notice and comprehend: A creature of nature. It would have to be a type of "shamanic" experience, or at least the illusion of one. If not, I might have missed whatever communication was circling around me. I was convinced that spirit, a higher power, that mysterious, yet ubiquitous ethereal entity that had permeated my life over the years, was seeking me as much as I was seeking It, Him, or Her. I was alive, alert, and awake to signs, messages, and guidance from the natural world, albeit not so much from the spiritual one. Now I was starting to try and put things together. Or, so I thought...

My life WAS changing! The year 2016-2017 culminated with a huge transformational shift in energy for me, I had an increased vitality, a lightening shock, an activation, with more fervor for all things metaphysical. All this and much more occurred in an abbreviated period with accelerated velocity. Red dragonfly had become my personal Ambassador of Change. But who WAS he? And what was this change? How would it look?

Finally, it wasn't me 'deciphering a code' of meaning in the red dragonfly visits, but more me physically, mentally, spiritually, and experientially assimilating my perception of the mission and message of the red dragonfly through visions, lucid dreaming,[10] and the soft summer breeze: Its breathless sigh, wordless speech, and silent serenade.

Red Dragon spoke to me, "*Live a life of love. Change what you must to live life on fire with passion & creativity. 'Show up' in your authenticity and let yourself get 'carried away' on the breezes of your heart's desires. In so doing, you recommit to your relationship with the Spirit. Also, you strengthen your relationship with yourself, your tribe, your community, the world, the universe, and the cosmos. Shed the old, be as if new; cleansed & pure. Recreate and be Who You Truly Are; One with the Spirit~Spirit loves through you as you spread Faith, Hope, Joy and magical blessings to all in need, and to all whom you touch, like the kiss of the dragonfly, one being at a time*" But whose voice was this, really? What exactly did it mean? Was it the beckoning of the universe? Some creative force? And who was this "Spirit?" Dragonflies are amazing and all, but I had come to see that it wasn't a simple dragonfly talking to me, it was some force speaking to me through the dragonfly. I know it sounds pretty weird, but even I, who is no stranger to weirdness, occasionally wondered about the source of this "voice."

The shedding hastened: It was ecstatically, electrifyingly, and euphorically accelerated. But Who was this Spirit?

Chapter 5

You've Got My Attention: Now What?

IN LATE AUGUST 2017, something odd happened. I was just about done for the day at work, trudging up the hospital steps to drop off my billing sheet for the patients I'd seen that day, when I saw a red dragonfly on the concrete steps, far away from water, marshes, or bogs. This is the hospital. A huge brick building, cement sidewalks, parking lots, asphalt, cars, concrete stairs, and NO red dragonflies. Yet there he was. How strange, I thought. I bent down to touch him figuring he'd fly away. He fluttered his wings but remained perched on the steps. I thought he must be injured or sick. I picked him up and held him for a bit, thinking about what to do next. I couldn't leave him to die alone on those barren hospital steps.

It was then that I had the startling, poignant, and compelling thought that felt almost inserted into my mind, "I don't want to die alone on these hospital steps, or in the sick, sad, increasingly toxic hallways of this place." The clear and present danger was never more apparent to me. Seeing *my* red dragonfly at *my* hospital, I knew I could die here if I allowed it, if I didn't make the necessary changes. Was this why he was there?

I carefully scooped him up, dropped off my billing sheet, grabbed a clean paper cup, and rode my bike home steering with my left hand, carrying Red in the cup in my right. Once home, laying on my bed, I placed Red on my bare stomach where we lay for a couple hours, quite still. I checked on him every so often while I read and relaxed. He did pass on about three hours after I'd initially found him. A friend told me she thought the red dragonfly came to me because he needed "a good death" and knew I wouldn't forsake him. Now I'm a Hospice for creatures.

Still, the irony never escaped me that he also may have sacrificed *his* life so that I would see and grasp the full meaning of *my* life in relation to my perception of my hospital job, my true purpose, and my potential impact on people's lives. Someone sacrificing their life for me didn't quite reach me that day, but it would later on. Was this a hint from Jesus?

I had always been very thankful for my job and for so many of the other wonders with which I'd been blessed. But this chain of events filled me with a new level of gratitude. This was a strange incident, the death of that little red dragonfly, which felt preordained. I felt "chosen." I was not used to that! Having never felt like I even belonged anywhere, now I was "chosen?" I began feeling that I belonged...somewhere. But where? And to what? Or to whom?

Just for the fun of experiment, one late October day in 2017, I went back to my old area at Bells Neck Reservoir on my bike to see if there were any red dragonflies there. This place, where I'd never seen one red dragonfly in all of 30 years, I figured would be devoid of them. They must be unique to my new area. What did I see right away? About TEN red dragonflies! They were all over the place. I, the skeptic, needed no more convincing. Red dragonfly blessed me by reminding me of what I'd nearly forgotten... *It's not just about me!* In fact, it's NOT about me AT ALL. It's 'we.' Everyone. Humanity. Community. *I Am/We Are.* Why privatize the Spirit?

After hours and days sitting with Red, his message and lesson became a little clearer. It wasn't just about career. In fact, it wasn't about career at ALL! It was so much greater than that. But what was it? Here I was in this weird limbo, betwixt and between—between the what was and the not yet. Liminal space is a concept described by Victor Turner in his study on initiation and ritual. The word liminal comes from the Latin word 'limen', meaning threshold – any point or place of entering or beginning. All transformation takes place in liminal space–on this holy ground; that season of waiting, and not knowing. If we're patient, we learn to wait and let this space form us. Nothing truly fresh or creative happens when we are inside our self-constructed comfort zones. Nothing original emerges from business as usual. It seems we need some "falling apart" for life to "fall together;" to give direction, depth, and purpose to our regular structure. Otherwise, structure, which is needed in the first half of life, tends to become a prison as we grow older.[11] I was in a holding pattern, and I was finally beginning to realize it.

It was about finding life's true meaning, finding joy, and finding my passionate purpose of magical blessings in my life and in every minute of every day. Then, passing this forward to others in love and service. Now that's Heavenly!!! In my hospital, I often felt like I was doing heavenly work. Sometimes I'd even say, "This is God's Work." But was it? And where to go now? And Who was this God to Whom I so casually referred?

There were still so many unanswered questions. WHO is Red Dragon? WHY is he calling *me*? For what, exactly, is he preparing me? One afternoon while I was thinking of this story, which I had inadvertently titled, "Lesson Of Red Dragon," it occurred to me, here in my liminality, I still had no idea what the lesson was! I felt suspended between two worlds, which wasn't a new feeling for me, but this undetermined, unresolved spiritual hanging fire was disconcerting to me. I felt pretty ignorant, frustrated even, that in my oblivious state I was missing some really important detail in the midst of the obvious. But what? Who? We don't know what we don't know. Looking back, this was true spiritual agitation. My blindness shielded me from a knowledge of God. So, in this case, a red dragonfly showed up, which would surely get my attention. And so he did.

Chapter 6

False Pride and Profound Unrest

IN 2015, I HAD started a side-business of aromatherapy, along with beginning my photography, plus my coaching. I was always seeking some avenue to help me escape from my hospital work. While I told myself I liked my medical career, I kept the secret hidden, especially to myself, that I had lost joy in it some time ago. What I still did enjoy was my title. I identified myself in my role of being a Medical Professional. I prided myself on my skills as an astute diagnostician, and my expertise for which I had become sought-after in the medical and psychiatric community. I had been an active participant long enough that I had become something of a consultant; younger doctors frequently asked my opinion. I served for ten years on the Psychiatric Consult-Liaison Team. I felt important and, at times, imperious. Essentially, I had for a long time been an egotistical creep who flaunted an alphabet soup of letters after my name, yet felt empty and abandoned inside.

Now, I wanted to be an "expert" in some different field, but I wasn't ready to let go of my accolades and self-perceived preeminence in my current one. If I could acquire the same prominence and distinction I held in the medical field in some new, but more glamorous, eclectic arena, I could jettison my medical career. My interests ranged from the New Age healing arts, to card-reading, to photography, to coaching. Coaching especially intrigued me, because I would teach everyone who felt disenfranchised or disillusioned in their current careers how they could have the great life that I was living, after leaving Medicine.

Of course, nothing could have been further from the truth. I had not left medicine, I felt disenchanted and embittered. The privilege of my title that I enjoyed in medicine was really a facade for how disappointed I was in myself. While thinking I had it all and appearing to be fabulously well-to-do in all areas of life, I felt a deep, inner desolation that all the spiritual juju, sparkle, and new age "love and light," could not assuage. I looked forward to the day when I would be coaching and not practicing medicine anymore, however, I had to first figure out how to support myself while making this transition. Being unemployed wasn't an option. Talk about being a big phony.

So, I persevered with this eclectic conglomeration of recently acquired side-gigs that I called a business, and I named it "Red Dragon Magic" after the red dragonfly. My website was "Red Dragon Magic," and I had offerings from aromatherapy products and services, Qigong, Tui Na, hedge-witchery,[12] astrology, coaching, photography, and more. Again, the naming of my new business venture was way before my knowledge of the Book of Revelation, or Jesus.

I even began to consider that maybe Red's message could be a "ministry." That word, ministry, came about from a man I met who had a "spirit walk" ministry website. I would never have thought of the word ministry on my own. Red Dragon Magic ~ The Ministry. I liked it. But, why magic, I wondered? And what actually is the difference between magic and miracles? And, what's a ministry, really? I'd never really given it much thought, as magic and miracles always seemed synonymous. I consulted several dictionaries which all concurred as to the actual difference between these two phenomena, and the differences far outweighed any similarity. In fact, the only connection between the two is, "One of the elements of both fairy tales (magic) and faith stories (miracles) is the supernatural. In fairy tales the supernatural is magical. In faith stories it is a miracle. Because the two seem very similar, it is easy to confuse magic and miracles."[13]

I now know a miracle is an amazing event caused by the power of God. It is from "above." Miracles are an act of God and rely on the will of God, are based on the power of God, and do not use energy. God usually works with the laws of nature (which He created), to perform the miraculous, yet He is free to work without, above, or against the laws of nature as well.

Magic is defined as a power that allows people to do impossible things with incantations or by performing special actions. Magic is an act of human beings and is also an act performed by humans. It is from "below," and in some instances can be demonic. It's a way to influence the world, like using symbols or rituals, with the manipulation of an object's nature, using present, available energy to impress itself upon its intended target(s). Magic "tricks" call for a magician's ability to organize methods to create some spectacle. In fact, it wouldn't surprise me if someone construed some scientific basis in a magician's compendium for a skillset to "create magic."

However, true magic, like Black magic, or the occult (think Ouija boards and the like), Satanic cults, some Haitian Voodoo are an incredibly dark energy, not to be fooled with, and clearly the work of the enemy. Ever notice how Haiti is continually besieged by natural disaster, unspeakable poverty, and misfortune? It may not surprise you to hear that

Haiti is under a demonic pact. You see, part of the Haitian national narrative, well known among Haitians and Haitian scholars alike, is the "Bwa Kayiman Vodou Congress" led by Boukman, who was a maroon escapee from a plantation and led a Vodou ceremony that was pivotal to the beginning of the Haitian Revolution (1791-1804). At this ceremony Boukman encouraged enslaved Africans to annihilate the plantation system of Colonial Haiti through the same violence that had been done to them.

On August 14, 1791, Boukman said these prophetic words, which C.L.R. James quotes in The Black Jacobins: "The god who created the sun which gives us light, who rouses the waves and rules the storm, though hidden in the clouds, he watches us. He sees all that the white man does. The god of the white man inspires us with crime, but our god calls upon us to do good works. Our god who is good to us orders us to revenge our wrongs. He will direct our arms and aid us. Throw away the symbol of the god of the whites who has caused us to weep, and listen to the voices of liberty, which speaks in the hearts of us all." Boukman, along with others, tore the Christian cross from their necks. Six days later, slaves led by Boukman massacred every white man, woman, and child they could find. This led to the Haitian Revolution and was the exact historical moment when Haiti was "consecrated to the Devil." Thus, Bwa Kayiman, by extension, ensured a legacy of misery in Haiti which we still see today (James.) This story was told to me by Haitian missionaries who believe, as many Haitians do, that this pact with Satan has sealed the fate of their country *(14)*.

The skill of a magician becomes evident in the act of magic. The power of God becomes evident in the act of miracles.

According to Merriam-Webster Dictionary, there is an actual word, Thaumaturgy, from the Greek, which means "magic;" the performance of miracles. The dictionary continues: "The magic of thaumaturgy is miraculous. The word, from a Greek word meaning "miracle working," is applicable to any performance of miracles, especially by incantation. It can also be used of things that merely seem miraculous and unexplainable, like the thaumaturgy of a motion picture's illusions (aka "movie magic"), or the thaumaturgy at work in an athletic team's "miracle" comeback. In addition to thaumaturgy, we also have thaumaturge, and thaumaturgic, both of which mean "a performer of miracles" or "a magician," and the adjective thaumaturgic, meaning "performing miracles" or "of, relating to, or dependent on thaumaturgy."[15] Merriam-Webster blew my contrast. Sometimes when we analyze something deeply, we end up more confused!

Still, to me the "magic" of nature, like the magic of a chrysalis becoming a butterfly, or the magical aeronautical maneuvers of the dragonfly, now seemed to be more miraculous than magic. So, be it magic or miracle, I believed a wonderful and important blessing was to come out of all this. I felt this, and it came to be true. Red dragonfly indicated that the more tools I had to spread blessings in people's lives, the better. Red told me, "*Our heart beats for all of humanity. We radiate our true love for all, and our Spirit of heartfelt wisdom IS the sacred miracle! We now can shine this light of love into the world, touching all and moving out in concentric circles from us, beyond us, beyond space and time.*" Even Red used both terms, so I concluded that perhaps one could have both without being mutually exclusive. Also, he may have used certain terms so I'd remain engaged.

OK. So, wait:

Radiating love? Shining a light? Isn't this what Jesus of Nazareth did? Spread love? Teach love? Be a beacon of light? I wasn't sure exactly what He did, honestly, but why did these thoughts just pop into my head? I was puzzled, however, later I would understand in retrospect so much more and recognize this as the start of Jesus' Great Commission.

Except, my version had left God out.

I hadn't really thought about Jesus, or God for that matter, other than an A.A. "higher power," but this was happening to me! With every person 'we' touch, our love grows larger, grander, brighter, stronger, filling the void within us. And what would that filled void look like? While still consciously unrecognized in myself, I clearly had a subconscious void. I'd catch a glimpse of it on rare occasions, but then I'd go off to fill any twinge of hollowness with a seminar, a man, a trip out in nature. There was this empty space in whatever part of me should have been filled with jubilance and the Holy Spirit. Here I wanted to lead by example, showing people how to have love, magic, hope, faith, and joy in their lives while I was yet to embrace these in my own. How duplicitous!

Chapter 7

Lucid Dreaming

IN A SUCCESSION OF lucid dreams from August to October 2017, I kept receiving messages; some invoked by my asking about a particular subject, and some seemingly random and unsolicited. They included a palpable frequency shift to a higher, lighter level, i.e., my body actually felt lighter. One of these dreams was of a rainbow, which I was actually within. It occurred in a clear blue sky, and I emerged as a woman with wings soaring over the world, and clutching a huge bouquet of different colorful flowers, of which all colors were unseen on the earthly plane. I morphed into a phoenix-like bird emerging from fiery ashes as I ascended through several dimensions in the heavens with varying densities. I was a part of the atmosphere, and I asked the Heavens how to best serve humanity. The answer came quickly, "Bloom where you're planted."

The next dream was that I was in a cave with many different animals. I was seeing everything in the cave through a narrow tunnel. Suddenly, I realized what the tunnel was; it was the barrel of a gun. I was sitting in it and I was the bullet! I was not discharged, but just sitting there in some kind of anticipation.

Next, I invoked Red Dragon and asked for direction. He greeted me and I received the message at the door of the cave entrance to "step over the threshold." I did, and heard myself say, "I'm in." as if prompted that I will await further instruction when it's time. Next, I see a white statue, so white it just about glows. I ask who it is. I get the symbol of a hand in a position I recognize as how Jesus' hands often appear in a statue form. At least, that was my interpretation. This was a statue of Jesus Christ. There was a shimmering, blazing light around the cave's entrance and in this moment, I knew it was Jesus, and He was waiting. I got chills.

Next, I also invoked my sister, Nancy, who died when she was young, and I asked her if she was in Heaven and what was it like? She said, "It's not what you think," in a non-reassuring tone. I felt it was very busy where we were, possibly a little disorganized, chaotic, dense, and loud. I tell her I am unclear as to what I'm experiencing. She clarifies, "It's harder than I thought." She showed me a deep emerald-green, lush garden with exotic tropical birds, and she indicated this could be my experience. It seemed like it could be different for each individual and hers wasn't so lovely, not unlike her life had been on earth. She was unsaved and had struggled with a partial-birth abortion when she was in her 20's, never forgiving herself.

I told her I wanted to speak to the part of me that has never belonged, the part that has always felt left behind, left out. She agreed to stay with me but suddenly I'm catapulted back to birth, in my mother's uterus with a cord wrapped around my neck. I felt stuck, even though there's a light in the distance. Then I somehow recall the cave, the light, the bullet: I am the bullet in the barrel of the gun, the baby in the birth canal, stuck. Waiting. I'm being choked and I'm filled with terror. In a flash, there was brightness, as if the faraway light just zoomed right up close and a thousand times brighter. I felt like basking in that light, but I'm not quite there, and also I felt left behind, as I had to stay in my infant body, in the darkness, in a holding pattern, strangled and suffocated, while also feeling isolated. I'm not sure where Nancy was yet, but it was ok.

But that light! That was what was so good. I didn't understand it, I just wanted it. The bullet in the barrel of a gun was about to be discharged, the baby in the birth canal finally was yanked out, and not without great turmoil. An enormous flood of very early childhood memories like a torrent engulfed me. I understood somehow the light was Heaven and I couldn't go there, I had to be left behind to live my life and in so doing, once I was "out" of the birth canal, I was "in" the world, yet with one foot still back "there," and one foot in earthly reality. Most of me was in the world for the long haul. That light, though....how I wanted to be in it.

Looking back, I considered what it was about the light that was so inviting. The closest I can come is to place myself emerging from a long, cold, dismal winter, and on one of the first sunny, warm, beautiful days of spring when the fragrance of Brugsmansia, Daphne, Wisteria, and then later, Lilacs fill the air, that feeling of the sun's warmth on my bare skin and enveloping my entire being in penetrating radiance is what the light was like. I hadn't even been born yet, but somehow I knew where I was going, represented a long dark nuclear winter, and the closer to it that I came, the further away from the light I became.

I had other lucid dreams and feelings of lightness, buoyancy, and a sparkling, glittery atmosphere with many layers like dimensions. There are so many more lucid dreams to tell about, many with mostly light, but some with dark symbolism. At the time, I did recognize some of the great signs of "Heaven" and of God or Jesus, and that of ascension, where I could feel myself literally traveling through heavier to lighter densities of atmosphere, always going higher. The other message I received on multiple occasions was that one of my gifts, and responsibilities, was clearly to "deliver and instill Faith in others." I just wasn't clear what this "gift and responsibility" meant, or from where the message came, or what this "faith" was. Faith in what? Or who?

I spent some time attempting to piece together the "religious" connotation of many of my lucid dreams, as if I was missing something. But what? I couldn't imagine, yet I understood more and more that my purpose was much greater and grander than I'd first surmised. Yet, I also knew it would be a very humble servitude with more service than I originally realized, and that this ministry and mission had something to do with spreading more love, hope, and faith in the world while giving up much of what I held dear, including my arrogance. The service I provided at my job was compensated very well monetarily. My reward was my title, my paycheck, and feeling good about myself because I was helping people: Not very altruistic. More and more I saw through myself; my pride, my ego, my pompous self-importance, and my supposed charitable generousness of spirit.

I wound down my role at the hospital, decreasing my hours. For a time, while rejoicing in God's work in my life, I continued my hospital job, but even working there part-time, I was well aware of being under a leadership which never ceased to remind me that we were all expendable and replaceable. Everything was about throughput, patient numbers, Press Ganey surveys, which is the tool used to measure healthcare quality assurance. Surveys are sent to patients who have been treated asking them their impressions about the hospital or healthcare facility, its staff, doctors, and nurses. Press Ganey gathers the data, runs the numbers, and then gives the information back to the hospital. We were schooled on keeping the survey scores high. And I get it. We want our patients to be satisfied. I'm not sure who talked the scores. All I knew was I belonged there even less. This theme of not belonging sure was becoming tiresome.

Chapter 8

One Wrong Choice Can Change Your Life Forever

O**NE DAY IN THE** ER, I was so overwhelmed and exasperated with approximately 45 patients assigned to me when I came on shift that morning at 0600. Having registered a complaint with my supervisor when she came in around 0900, and she ignored or dismissed my plight, I essentially signed off on a couple patients without completely assessing them. In medicine, this is poor practice–malpractice, to be exact. Right at that moment, I had a twinge of intuition that this was a turning point, a significant lowering of my personal practice standards. "This is bad," I told myself. This moment would weigh heavily with immense gravity on my life going forward. I had no idea just how, or to what degree. I only felt the profundity in my psyche that this one moment, this one choice, would change my life forever.

Over the following months, aside from our health care system devolving, spending less time with patients and more time documenting on a computer, I felt I was sacrificing too much of my time and that of my patients. Was this what I'd gone to school for? At that same time, I learned of a complaint that had been filed by a RN who worked with me on that fateful day that I documented on those patients who I saw, but did not thoroughly truly "see," or completely assess. As this reverberated through the hierarchal channels, it finally came to a head. Before I could bow out on my own, in March 2018, I was forced to resign from my NP position/career of 20 years. I was shocked. The RN had reported me to the head of their nursing union, who, in turn, reported me to the Board of Registration, from where my license comes. No patient had been harmed, I told myself, nor had the RN, except she felt I wasn't helping her with some difficult psychiatric patients who were acting out that day. I completely understood her position and couldn't blame her. Lots happened in those 10 hours of my shift. No one felt supported that day, I just had no one to whom I could report—no union or union rep. Still, my failure to accept ownership of my error ultimately resulted in far-reaching remorse down the road over my lack of courage around admission of my own wrongdoing. Knowing what I know now, I would have never responded as I did. I would have gone directly to the Chief

Medical Officer, who was a really nice guy and if I had come completely clean as to what I'd done and why, maybe my job might have been saved. Why didn't I? It was like I had a gag order. I just didn't advocate for myself at all. I didn't even throw my immediate supervisor, the Chief of Staff of my department, who wasn't helpful under the bus. As it turned out, she was terminated too, and I don't know why to this day.

Still, I believe this was God working in me. I should have left this job earlier, and in my life what I do not discard, God takes away from me. He does it for me, just not always in a way I might prefer.

Nothing happened for a couple years, so I went on to work three days per week in a much less stressful addictions facility, where I was confined to a small, closed office, writing prescriptions all day. I felt I had finally been gifted with time to fully and completely pursue my blessed, magical, passionate purpose. But what was it? And where? And how?

I feel I have always been equipped to "function" in the spiritual realm of dreams and symbolism and have been allowed to stretch my wings. Nothing on this earth can compete with the sheer joy of breathing life into people physically, but also giving them life mentally and spiritually with hope, faith, love, and showing them a new way of being, as we do working with addicts seeking recovery. I wasn't entirely aware at the time, yet in all this and more, Red dragonfly had been quietly coaching me, preparing me and guiding me.

Of course, there were many red dragonflies I suppose, however, this specific "form" of a red dragonfly persisted over years. I am sure there could be copious debates about this "form" of being and how it could persist for so long. Just like scholars will always debate among themselves, inhabiting disparate worlds of thought, there is often some strong consensus regarding meaning and message. In this instance, I'm not talking about the phenomenality or ontology of momentary things or how transient things can become enduring things; this dragonfly was a study in both change and persistence....and he was real. As for his message and meaning, revelation would come.

Chapter 9

Andy

I BEGAN GOING BACK IN my memory to what I was doing in my life besides working as a NP around the time of meeting the red dragonfly. In early 2015, as I said earlier, my mother died. Right around this time, I had been dating a man briefly who, after knowing each other for three weeks, had asked me to marry him. I declined. Later that same year, I met another man who asked me to marry him within a month of knowing him. I again declined. What was *that* all about, I wondered? My sexual history had been filled with instances of promiscuity, followed by a celibate four or five years of associating with no man. I was almost always in relationships of brief serial monogamy if I was in any at all. While I had encountered several possibilities for a partner among men I had met, the pool of potential mates was relatively small. Also, I sought perfection, so if things didn't work out (they never did), I had a reason to ghost on them. It was mid-summer of 2015, amidst knowing both these men who had proposed, Red came into my life as an obvious messenger. My mother's passing was sad, but it was expected. She was 93 years old. There were the usual funeral tasks to accomplish, which I was able to do with my daughter Christine's help, as I had been preparing for Mom's death for some time.

A year later, in the summer of 2016, I clearly recall being out in the bog and asking "spirit" or "the universe" for a companion; someone to share my beautiful surroundings with. The more I had gotten to know red dragonfly, my thoughts of promiscuity had subsided a little, and instead, I began wishing for just one man to share nature with. He would be a man who loved nature as much as me. That very day, several hours later, I met a man out in the middle of the woods while I was frolicking about taking photos in the bog. He said he lived on the edge of this same cranberry bog I'd visited countless times, yet I never saw him before. Still, on this day we literally almost ran into each other and struck up a conversation. At first, I was slightly unnerved about being scantily clad in the woods with an unknown man three feet away. Still, we had a detailed conversation for an hour, then we parted ways. The whole time I was sitting on a log, with Red sitting right next to me. I asked at the end of our conversation if he was married, and he replied, "barely."

I figured most married men would downplay their marriage when meeting a bikini-clad woman in the woods, so I wrote him off even though he seemed like the "nature man" I was seeking. For the next several weeks he kept "finding" me out in the woods. He knew everything about the outdoors. He had made many of the trails I had walked on in the bog himself and could tell me the names of all the trees, plants, and birds in the bog. He was well-versed in all matters of nature, having worked out in it most of his life.

He later told me he could tell when I was in the bog because when he was in his yard mowing the lawn or gardening, red dragonflies would suddenly "show up," which he said he hadn't really noticed very much until he met me. He said every time ten or fifteen came, landing on his shed or on him, he felt like they were telling him I was in the bog so he would go there immediately, because he knew I'd be there. And I was usually cavorting with my red dragonfly friends. Nonetheless, I couldn't shake the knowledge that he purposely hunted me. I wasn't freaked out about it; it was just an observation to be noted and logged.

When I asked him if he ever came to the bog in the evening, he told me that his wife would never allow that. Perplexed, I asked him why, and he told me "We never go out after dinner." This was a *very* married man, not a barely married man. He told me he had been married for 34 years with the last 15 of it being "unhappy," coinciding with his only son moving out of the family home. With his son gone, he and his wife apparently had little in common, so he spent time working, doing yard work, and completing home improvements. One evening, once I figured out where he lived, I drove by his home and of all the homes on the street, his was the most meticulously kept and the best-maintained home and yard. He wasn't kidding about his pastime. Both their vehicles were parked neatly in the driveway, a representation of the perfect couple.

I initially resisted his subtle sexual advances, this man who identified himself to me as Alexander. Even though I had heard him tell me his name, after a week or two I'd heard his name in my mind to be "Andy." I called him that once early on, and he said, "What? Hey that's my family name!" He smiled curiously, "My mother nicknamed me Andy when I was little. How'd you know that?" I didn't of course, it just came out like that because I had transposed his name somehow in my dyslexic mind. This would be the first of many odd coincidences that would occur between Andy and me.

Sometimes Andy would come upon me when I was visiting with red dragonfly and I was not amused, because to me, times with my red dragonfly were more important than times with him or anyone. Over time, Andy began to grow on me, even though I really didn't see any future for us.

I liked him well enough, but I wasn't crazy over him. Still, we walked through the woods, held hands, kissed, and he told me about his life and his unhappiness with his wife. I felt a closeness and yes, even intimacy along with physical attraction. Perhaps there was even an element of feeling like I could be "better" than his wife and even though sometimes I felt like "all the good ones were taken," maybe there was some chance for us. His wife from his description, sounded quite dull, and I knew in my heart that I was anything but. Yet, I told myself that this man, this twin flame,[14] as it were, would just be a "fling," and nothing serious. He'd be short-lived. As it turned out, as usual, things unfolded differently than I'd imagined.

I definitely had ominous feelings about a married man, even without being a Christian. I tried to work with Andy at first, suggesting things he might try with his wife to possibly rekindle their relationship, thinking perhaps I might be a catalyst to reuniting them. It didn't take long for me to realize Andy wasn't having it, and maybe neither was she. I felt bad "stealing" another woman's husband, like I was violating a sacred feminine alliance. Yet, the more I heard about her, the less I felt this. Still, I realized I was hearing of her through Andy's lens. Almost everything I'd learned about her eventually turned up to be true. Andy later told me that he had never really loved her. They were young and marriage

Andy

just seemed like "the thing to do," however, it had long outlived its usefulness.

My heart was becoming captivated by this simple, yet kindred spirit of a man. A man who adored being out in nature and seemingly adored me. Eventually, as winter approached, and Red was less accessible, I stopped going to the bog. After about three days of my not being out there, I was sitting on my front steps when Andy "showed up" at my house. We sat on the steps outside. This happened on several occasions and I'm not going to lie, it was just a little creepy; stalker-like, as I had never told him where I lived. But my lack of self-esteem also found it flattering. I'm not sure why I didn't let him in my house other than I felt like it was crossing some kind of line. In retrospect, this was twisted logic when we had already been swept away in the deep blue seas of August out in the bog and known each other intimately outside in late summer's lush green grasses and sun-soaked fields.

Finally, on one late autumn day, I invited him inside. I admit I felt guilty about being with him romantically from the start, as I was aware of violating another woman's sacred connection with her husband and while not being well-versed in the ten commandments, I knew full well what they were, and we were committing adultery. Still, amidst this admission, I experienced something I've never had before, except with my own two children. At the doorway of my house as

Andy was leaving after one of the first times he'd come by, we embraced for a couple of minutes, and as we did, I felt my heart literally open up wide, just like I imagine a flower's petals unfolding in slow motion and opening up, and accompanied with a sense a great warmth. Maybe because his heart and mine were against each other, chest-to-chest, but I felt a most electric, warm opening that can only be described as love.

This isn't a single, consecutive unfolding, but rather an opening that spans the depth of dimensions; it can't be quantified or qualified. It's kind of like a linear versus the vertex form of a quadratic function, multidimensional and free of carnality. The only way it can be known and felt is experientially. When I have embraced my children when they were little, on many occasions a similar feeling enveloped my heart. With other people, a lesser version of this feeling had occurred, but I don't recall it ever happening with a man to this intense of a degree; one really doesn't forget such a feeling. What in the world was that? Perhaps a glimpse of what could be? Or what is?

Now, I know what you're thinking, and I completely understand. How can a love so seemingly pure be borne out of adultery? Believe me, I questioned this myself over and over. I even tried to renounce it, telling myself it wasn't true, it didn't really happen, but it really did. So, I still don't have a clear resolution or reconciliation. All I can do is describe this profound experience of unconditional, agape love that surrounded me, and us, on that afternoon.

I reasoned that this liaison would end, and I told him so. I was planning to go to Florida and said perhaps we'd meet up next spring or summer in the bog. I was fully prepared to cut him loose. It was a few days later, in late October, when I fully realized he was that companion I had asked for and what is sometimes referred to as a twin flame. I didn't feel like we were soulmates; that may have been a designation for he and his wife….an old, comfortable relationship. No, I felt a longing for him I hadn't felt for anyone since my twenties. Was it because he was taken? I wasn't sure. In retrospect, I understood that we were both traveling a frequency, which would have brought us together; a frequency which we had both probably unknowingly traveled for a very long time.

According to an article I read on the subject by Janet Brito,[16] both twin flames and soulmates can occur in either romantic or platonic relationships, including between family members. While these relationships seem similar on the surface, they're not the same. Twin flames are seen as a soul that's been split in two. Soulmates are two separate souls coming together in a way that feels destined.

Brito continues, that while twin flames are often mirror images, soulmates often complement each other; twin flames are more like kindred spirits. Soulmate relationships tend to feel very comfortable and supportive. Twin flame relationships, on the other hand, tend to be the opposite, catapulting one or both people into unchartered realms.

> "They come into your life and expose all the things that were issues for you: your traumas or growth edges, and most people feel their world has been completely upended" (Brito).

This can lead to personal awakening, or disaster.

From what I understand, twin flames are often there because they're supposed to be part of your growth and healing and teach you something, but people may overlook the unhealthy side of these relationships.

We don't want to see certain features in ourselves because we're so attracted to the other person and feel so connected, which can lead to codependency or boundary crossing. "Where do they end and you begin? That's not usually the case with a soulmate" (Brito).

Meanwhile, he continued to describe to me how unhappy he had been over the last fifteen years of his "barely married" life and continued to affirm that he never was in love with his wife, and actually had been involved with a brief affair some ten years earlier. I was leaving for Virginia Beach for

Andy

Thanksgiving and he stopped over to say goodbye, but before he left just before he turned to walk away, he paused, turned to me and said, "I love you." I realized I had come to love him too and was relieved when he said it. No one wants to be the single woman telling the married guy she loves him, but he said it first. I recall asking him if he was ready to have his life changed forever? He replied without hesitation that he was. I asked if he was willing to jump blind-folded into the abyss? He again said he was. *What was I even talking about?* I don't know, but I was sure he would undergo the transformation of a lifetime, and it seemed voluntary on his part. He could just go home and forget all this ever happened, but he said he wanted change and he wanted me.

We could never have imagined what would follow.

Andy and I became a monogamous couple. He left his wife, his home, and everything he had worked so hard for over the past 34 years of his marriage, hoping to be with me, although on my end, there were no promises, no guarantees, and in this I was transparent. Andy said he had "a good feeling that we would stay together." I wasn't so sure. I hadn't given up much of anything, other than him moving in with me. Whereas he had given up his entire world as he had always known it.

What on earth have I done, I asked myself. Over time, I wracked my brain over why this whirlwind of emotional attachment and overt sexual desire that was also sprinkled with a pureness of love had overtaken me for this married man. While I had been a "free spirit" since I was in my teens, with the exception of a brief marriage and a couple of seven-year-long relationships, I had lived alone. In truth, the term "free spirit" referred to my powerful sexual nature and was actually just another way to describe my immorality. I never really saw it that way while in the throes of it. Much later, I realized and finally understood that I, besides being an alcoholic and a drug addict in recovery all those years, was also addicted to relationships. I just never recognized it as such. Serial monogamy. I can't believe I never saw it! Furthermore, I thought that this was an aspect of myself that had calmed down somewhat, as compared with my younger years. However, like any true addiction, until you face the demon it doesn't subside at all, and if anything, it actually seemed even more intense with Andy. It had just existed in a quieter place as I had been keeping to myself and ignoring or avoiding the beast, except perhaps in my fantasies.

Andy proved to be both a desirous and a wretched companion, as he went through a very long, messy divorce from an angry wife and he eventually lost everything. We saw the true meaning of the saying, "Hell hath no fury like a woman scorned." We were still "in love," with a closeness that I recognized as both a physical and emotional connection. But it was during this tumultuous time that I acknowledged to myself that nothing good could come from what Andy and I had done. In Andy's struggles with the divorce attorneys and his soon-to-be ex-wife, I felt hemmed in by all this strife and could not see anything truly positive, even once Andy was "free." He was changed by it all, and no longer the carefree nature guy I had fallen for. During his divorce, he had also developed a bad drinking problem, which one could question whether he had it before. His married life seemed pretty dull, and he appeared to be well-trained in husbandly matters. Still, I suspect he drank in secret, and in denial, when the wife was busy sewing or watching TV.

Chapter 10

Saved!

IN 2018, A GREAT miracle occurred, which helped me make more sense of this 5-year odyssey, while still leaving more questions unanswered. While I was calling this story the Lesson of Red Dragon before I'd finished writing it, I STILL didn't know what the lesson was! And who was Red Dragon?

I don't even know why, but I'd begun listening to Christian satellite radio over the summer of 2018 as my new addictions job required a commute. I loved the various preachers and their messages, which were moving me more and more. I started traveling off-Cape to visit with my daughters, both of them having recently moved to the South Shore of Massachusetts. I kept hearing a "Pastor Randy" preaching the Word of God. I was always mesmerized by his voice and his expository teaching style when he came on at 5:30pm. He always had a message and it often seemed to pertain to me.

Saved!

One day, driving down the road leaving Rockland, having left the sober house where one of my daughters was living, a radio Pastor with a southern accent asked if I was lost (as if he were speaking right to me), and if so, to just say a prayer in a 'repeat-after-me' format. It was basically what I came to know as a sinner's prayer, as follows: "Jesus, I confess that I am a sinner, and I am lost. I can't continue this way and today, I commit my life to You, Jesus; I confess that I believe that you, Jesus Christ are my one true Savior and my Lord, and that you died on the cross, sinless, so my sins are forgiven. I repent of all my sins and today I commit my life to You, Lord, and I ask to be saved in the name of Jesus Christ ~ Amen."

I was able to repeat it all and by the end, tears were streaming down my face. There I am, barreling down the expressway at 75mph, bawling my eyes out! I'd never forgotten about all my life's transgressions, having broken every one of God's commandments, and thus, not feeling worthy. Still, I never truly, entirely forgot God either. So, having prayed that prayer of salvation, I finally had some sense of relief. Even with the elation I had felt from my sittings with Red, there was still a piece of the mystery that I was missing, and I felt like he–or someone–was just waiting patiently for me to finally "catch on." But to what? To *THIS!!!* These saving words repeating the sinner's prayer opened floodgates of emotion, a gushing of tears, waves of regret, heart-felt repentance and regeneration, rapturous rejoicing, and then, peace.

I continued to listen to Pastor Randy on the radio, who in contrast to many of the southern-sounding Pastors, had a noticeable Boston accent. One day I discovered that he was the Pastor of Calvary Chapel in Rockland–right down the street from where my daughter Catie was living! I can't really explain why I had begun going to church–maybe just looking for something? I'd recently been attending Calvary Chapel on Cape Cod, seeking to learn more about the Word, and hoping to find whatever I was seeking; to assuage the spiritual unrest I'd been feeling. Coincidence? Or Divine appointment? Calvary Chapel! Now I HAD to go find Pastor Randy's Calvary Chapel. I HAD to hear him in person.

One Sunday I drove up to Rockland, an hour from my home, and found Calvary Chapel on Market Street. There he was. Pastor Randy. He sounded just like he did on the radio. His sermon was all about Mercy. Of course! It was one of those sermons where you want to ask, "How did he know? Is this just for me?" He cited at least fifteen biblical passages from scriptures of Old & New Testaments where God speaks of Mercy. Being a sinner, the Mercy theme struck me in a powerful way I can't quite explain, other than admission of all my sins for so many years, resisting God, running rogue, and worshipping false idols. Flashing before me were my many years of feeling broken, unworthy, never belonging anywhere, never being good enough for anything or anyone, much less good enough to ever enter the Kingdom of God. Could I finally belong?

It's as if the Holy Spirit Himself grabbed me head-on by both shoulders, shook me and said, "LISTEN UP!!!"

I did.

Then, the most amazing thing of all happened: The alter call. Pastor Randy asked if anyone in the crowd needed to be saved. I'm thinking, yup, that would be me, even though I felt partially saved that day driving, praying, and crying in my car. Then he waited. I hesitated. As if he knew there was someone out there who was on the fence, he added, "If God came down to judge you today, would you be able to bow at his feet?" I was thinking, "Heck, no!"

Red dragonfly had been painstakingly preparing me for something, but I hadn't expected this. A voice whispered to me, "If you leave here today without going up there, you're going to regret it more than you can know! Don't leave without this! Get up there!!!" Ugh. I wanted to crawl under the pew, not stand naked and exposed at the alter in front of all those people. Yet, I just knew I'd be filled with remorse if I didn't.

I stood up, walked my bad self up to the alter while a few people gleefully clapped, and I stood in front of Pastor Randy.

Wow. Was this really happening? Pastor Randy prayed a sinner's prayer like the Pastor had done on the radio and I repeated it. I couldn't believe it! I felt dissociated from my body. The whole congregation was now wildly clapping and cheering! Pastor Randy then directed me to go with one of the other pastors to get a free Bible and some instructions. It was a bit surreal, but I did what I was told. Fortunately, when I returned we weren't done yet! There was monthly communion! I was shocked! First, I finally got to hear Pastor Randy preach, and second, he spoke all about Mercy ~ TODAY of all days, as if just for me, a miserable sinner! Then third, I got SAVED!!! Finally, I received Holy Communion.

Somehow, when you accrue so many sins, you just don't feel right receiving Holy Communion, so it had been decades for me since the last time I did. But they said it was okay. I left Calvary that day elated, euphoric, and full of the Spirit. I remember texting Andy, saying, "Open your heart, Everything is love!" We'd been separated for a while, but I felt I had to share that. Meanwhile, with that coming out of nowhere he must've wondered what was up. But my heart was bursting with unconditional love. I can't remember ever feeling this way before. It was like a strange and wonderful drug, except it wasn't a drug. It was the Holy Spirit. I did know that much.

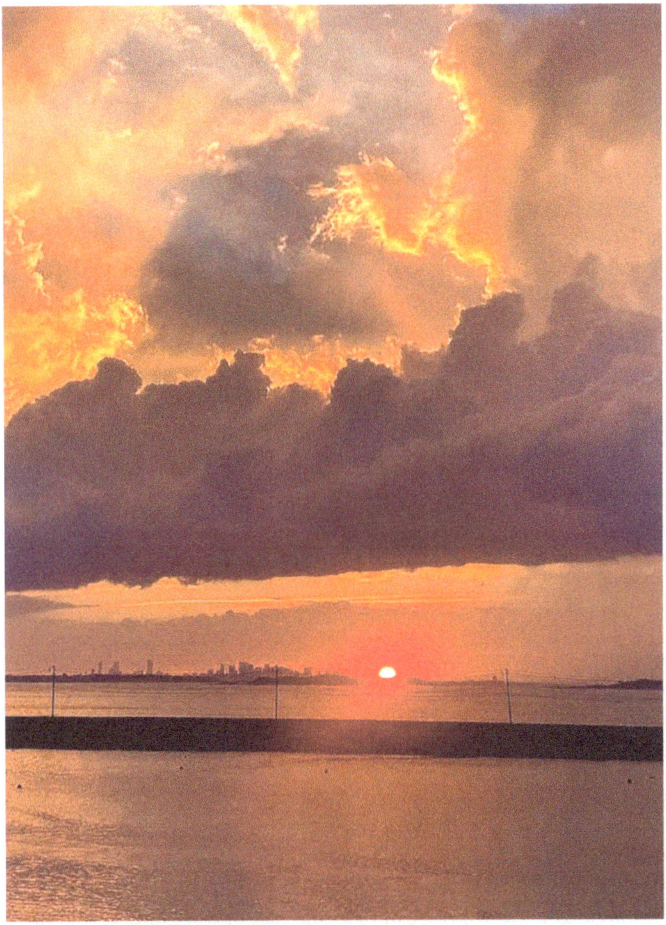

Chapter 11

Return to El Bethel

IN THE BIBLE THERE is a story about Jacob. God wanted Jacob to go to where he had first become right with God at Bethel, a name which infers separation from sin, and fellowship with God. "Bethel" means House of God–a place of solitude and intimacy with Him. Jacob had left his homeland because his brother, Esau sought revenge against Jacob for tricking him out of his own birthright. While camped at a place he called Bethel, God revealed Himself in a dream to Jacob while he slept. After that special encounter with God at Bethel, Jacob made a vow to God, saying, If God will be with him, and keep him in the way that he goes, and make provisions for him, so that he returns again to his father's house in peace; then shall the Lord be my God (Genesis 28:20-21). Having granted Jacob his plea to Him, God reminded him about his vow in Genesis 28:20. Jacob acknowledged his vow and said to his household, "And let us arise, and go up to Bethel; and I will make there an altar unto God, who answered me in the day of my distress, and was with me in the way which I went" (Genesis 35:3). Later, upon heading back to his homeland, Jacob encountered and wrestled all night with an angel or spirit of God, telling his spiritual opponent that he wouldn't stop until he received God's blessing. After Jacob received his desired blessing, he came out wounded at his hip. The sun rose and Jacob was given the new name, Israel, which means "he who wrestles with God." This name reflects his struggle, and the destiny of the nation of Israel. Jacob had become right with God, but not without a struggle, and a price–his life-long hip injury (Genesis 32:22–32; Hos. 12:3–5). Jacob couldn't go part-way, he had to go back to the beginning and start from there, his home (Gen. 35:1-12 NIV). I sensed that this peculiar "homecoming," was also my mission.

Where had I encountered God before? Where had I experienced Him before I fell from His Grace? Really, was I ever even IN God's grace? In a flash of memories, I returned to when I was in my early 20's and had found some inkling of God when I got sober. I was walking what I suppose back then was a righteous path, in some sort of touch with Him, going to A.A. and working the steps, believing in a "higher power." I thought I was in God's will. Was I? How had I forgotten what I thought I once knew? Perhaps I had never really known? I had known all the words and sung all the notes, but I never quite learned the song. God knew all the answers to the questions I didn't even know to ask.

I had gone to church regularly for a while when I was 23 years old. I met and married a good friend in my early 20's and we had our wedding ceremony in the Catholic Church for his Irish Catholic parents' sake. Less than two years later, I would leave that marriage because I wasn't ready to settle down or sleep with the same man for the rest of my life. I remember having a vague premonition that this would be one of those decisions that would alter the course of my life forever. Funny how in my life I knew ahead of time a certain move on my part would negatively affect my course, and in the face of it, I would turn a deaf ear, or a blind eye. Indeed, it did change things, as my life after that was never the same. Like a broken plate that can be glued together, but never again is it as it was; never again is it pristine, perfect. I resorted to drinking heavily again after four years of being clean and sober and was living like an outlaw on the outskirts of town; homeless, drunk, becoming that person parents warn their kids about.

Had I backslidden? Or had I never grasped God in the first place? Had I deviated so far from God's Way? And with each deviation, like an algorithm of sin, had I become exponentially further and further away from God? Or did

I ever really even know Him? Knowing what I know now, I would have to say no. My attitude about God was that of a casual acquaintance. I didn't really *know* Him. I wasn't in an intimate love relationship with Him, nor did I know or have any concept of a relationship with Jesus Christ. What I now know about God is that He simply cannot and will not settle for casual. He accepts no compromise. I was all about compromise, negotiation, bargaining, the middle road, the wide gate. "Enter by the narrow gate; for wide is the gate and broad is the way that leads to destruction, and there are many who go in by it" (Matt. 7:13 NKJV). Yes, my "gate" was wide open alright.

It occurred to me that I had never even read the Bible, nor did I know His Holy Word. I knew that I had never walked in, after, or with The Spirit. In fact, I wasn't aware of the Holy Spirit at all. What the Father has devised for us, the Son has accomplished for us, and now the Holy Spirit communicates it to us. By our steadfast obedience to the Holy Spirit, we keep open the way for Him to impart it to us. This is His ministry. He has come for this very purpose–that He may make real in us all that is ours through the finished work of Christ. "The Holy Spirit of God is within me, to open to me the Scriptures so that I may find Christ there, to direct my prayer, to govern my life, and to reproduce in me the character of my Lord."[17]

Over the course of years, decades, I became so estranged from God, that I never prayed, and no longer really even remembered Him. I rarely gave a thought to Him and never to Jesus, but then again, I hadn't really learned who Jesus was, so I didn't have a relationship with Him or understand the significance of who He truly was, and is.

I understood the concept of sin, the Ten Commandments, the idea of mortal sin and all of us being doomed to sin by the disobedience of one man, Adam. Never did I even entertain the miraculous undoing of this by Jesus Christ; not through my meager knowledge derived from Catholicism, nor from my complete lack of general spiritual understanding. This Jesus, Who, upon the Cross, through His obedience, we were/are saved. I completely missed the memo. All we had to accept was that we were crucified with Him on that Cross upon Golgotha. The Book of Romans, by Apostle Paul, so beautifully, yet heartbreakingly, tells the story. "O wretched man that I am! Who will deliver me from this body of death?" (Rom. 7:24 NKJV) Paul laments that "For I do not understand what I am doing; for I am not practicing what I want to do, but I do the very thing I hate" (Rom. 7:15 NASB).

Straight away, Paul goes on to explain that Jesus Christ lived on earth as all man and all God, and died here for our sin, doing for us that which we couldn't do for ourselves. God's law was fulfilled, and justice done for our transgressions.

When we come to faith in Christ, we live according to God's Holy Spirit, not by our flesh. Those in the flesh (the world's way of living for self before and above all else) are estranged from God (Rom. 8:1–8). Jesus gave the ultimate sacrifice for us and all we need to do is claim it in faith. This revelation brought me to tears on more than a few occasions.

I could sure relate to Paul's "wretched man" statement. I had lived forty wretched years, although not without doing and experiencing some very good things. But those good deeds were for whom? While I was seemingly selfless, I knew the answer. It was, in the end, always about me. I had managed to raise my incredible daughters, attain two master's degrees, save lives, and yet it was all self-directed. I had something to prove, and I was not going to rest until I became "someone." The world belongs to Satan, the Prince of the Powers of the Air (2 Cor. 4:4). I was a daughter of disobedience, akin to Satan. I had danced with Satan throughout much of my life. I had accrued monetary wealth and the thought of divesting myself of it, or the means by which to earn it, was absolutely foreign to me. My money and assets had become my identity, my god. Jesus once told a parable of a rich man who couldn't leave his wealth to follow Jesus, adding, "It is easier for a camel to go through the eye of a needle than for a rich man to enter the Kingdom of God!" (Matt. 19:24 NASB). So, to give that up I would need a smaller camel or a larger needle.

Finally the shedding could now truly begin. God's Holy Spirit lives in every Christian who has been born again. "It is easier for a camel to go through the eye of a needle than for a rich man to enter the Kingdom of God" (John 3:3 ESV). The Spirit, given to us by God, is the same Holy Spirit that raised Christ from the dead.

He will resurrect us as well, after these sin-drenched bodies have died. Never had I truly understood the concept of dying to be reborn. I had heard the term, "born again," as applied to what I thought were crazed, Bible-waving Christians, but this was the first time after my Calvary experience that I truly understood it from an experiential perspective. Not only did I know it from hearing scripture, but I FELT it. Even though we are warned not to go by feelings alone, I did feel it, however it was also supported by my eventual scrutiny of the Old and New Testaments of the Holy Bible. Like Snake said, "be as if new." The shedding was taking on new meaning, with the words of Apostle Paul who said, "You were taught, with regard to your former way of life, to put off your old self, which is being corrupted by its deceitful desires" (Eph. 4:22 NIV).

The heartbreaking story of Nicodemus, only told in the Gospel of John, describes Nicodemus, a Pharisee and member of the royal Sanhedrin. He was a prominent, elitist Jewish Rabbinical leader and teacher. He came to Jesus furtively at night, so not to be discovered, and said, "I know that you are one that is sent, for no one who is not sent by God could do the things that you do." Jesus explained about being born again, "Truly, truly, I say unto you, unless one is born from above, he cannot enter the Kingdom of God. That which is born of the flesh is flesh, and that which is born of the spirit is spirit. Marvel not that I have said unto you that you must be born from above, for I tell you that the wind blows where it wills, and you hear the sound of it, but you cannot tell whence it comes nor whither it goes. So is everyone who is born of the spirit" (John 3:1-21).

Nicodemus couldn't understand. When Jesus said, "born again", Nicodemus saw only physical birth, somehow returning to his mother's womb, which was, of course, impossible. Jesus explained that the birth can't be of the flesh, for flesh and blood can't inherit the Kingdom of God, nor enter it. Only Spirit can, for God is Spirit. Nicodemus finally came to believe and wanted to follow Jesus but he was afraid of losing his status. Later on, after Jesus' death, he actually helped tend to Jesus' body at the tomb. He was driven from the Temple by his fellow Pharisees. I felt like Nicodemus; unable to shake my persona at first, then later being sold-out on fire for Jesus. I was determined to make everything right, to do whatever it took. It's incredible the effect Jesus has on us to this very day.

Jacob didn't just encounter God at El Bethel, he was transformed by Him. He originally arrived with the price of sin on his head, engaged in a struggle, and left with what he believed to be God's confirmation that he was chosen, and would therefore follow God, encouraged by a future full of the hope of a saved man.

So, as Jacob was instructed to do by returning to El Bethel, I too knew I had to go back to before, to when I last felt even remotely close to God. Back to when I was twenty-three years old.

Chapter 12

Forty Years of Wilderness Wandering: Recovery

FLASHBACK TO THE 1970'S: I knew at a very young age that I had a problem with alcohol. Growing up where liquor was abundant and enthusiastically encouraged, I had free rein to drink almost daily if I wished, starting at 6 or 7 years old. By the age of 18, I admitted to myself that I was a full-blown alcoholic, "and I'm gonna die this way" I told myself one night standing before a mirror. Despite many brushes with the law, a psychiatric hospitalization, and briefly being a ward of the state all by 16 years old, it wouldn't be until 5 years after my admission to myself I was an alcoholic that I actually quit drinking. My peculiarities growing up, my sensitivity to everything, the feeling of not belonging, and my extra-intuitiveness left me always on the outside of life, with a foot in two different worlds. Even with admitting my own alcoholism, I would still continue the madness until I was 23, almost physically dying, and most certainly spiritually dead.

Finally, as they say in A.A., I was "sick and tired of being sick and tired." When I quit drinking on May 30th, 1977, I began attending random A.A. meetings with a sponsor named Shirley B. Shirley was a woman in her 50's from the small town where I lived, and I wasn't really sure what it was all about. I was living in a house with two drug addicts who had cocaine, heroin, and at times, Percodan that they would cold-shake and shoot. But IV coke or heroin was the most featured drug at the time of my newly-found sobriety, and it seemed like a good thing to try, since I had tapered myself off alcohol and was "getting sober." I really didn't understand the concept of recovery back then. I certainly didn't make the connection between drugs and alcohol and that it's all the same!

Within two weeks of quitting drinking, eating all the chocolate I could from Ring-Dings to Devil Dogs to chocolate bars, I commenced to shoot coke and opiates. This developed into a raging drug habit with cravings that could never be quelled. Any further attempt at A.A. went out the window. Life with alcohol couldn't compare to life with drugs. They wore off way too fast and my life rapidly became consumed by a frenzied obsession—the obsession and compulsion to get more dope, to procure more money with which to buy it, to optimize my own personal talents for luring it away from the dealer that was selling it without any monetary exchange, or to acquire it myself for sale, with the plan for some left over to use. This never worked, of course, as I'd just shoot it all. However, it was still never, ever enough. With my addiction raging, I would have to chase that high like a starving lion chases its prey. Like the Greek myth of Sisyphus who was doomed to repeatedly push a boulder up a hill for all eternity, it was a task that would never end. It was always a moving target, forever swirling turbulently ahead of me, faster and farther away from my grasping hands and my broken heart. I had been conspicuously resourceful in obtaining alcohol, but nothing could compare to the unabashed and undignified manipulation of my own personal assets to procure drugs.

Somehow, in the heat of all this drug activity and the deleterious effect it was having on my physical and mental being, I had some sense that this was not the path I wanted to choose in my "sobriety." Still, I just couldn't stop. In fact, I kept using more, because I had to. It took more and more to satisfy me, which of course it never did, much like the trajectory of alcohol but exponentially faster, and, there was just never enough. After so many months of my drug extravaganza, I found myself in a drug-induced catatonia; death-like.

I understood the concept of overdose, and I was pretty sure I was dying. Lying on a bed one day, I was unable to move any part of my body. No part of me was functioning, with the exception of scant, shallow breaths, labored and terminal. My mind was wafting in and out of consciousness. My breathing was making a gurgling sound and I couldn't clear my throat. I don't know, or recall, how much coke and dope I'd shot leading up to this state, but I was in and out of consciousness for what seemed like eternity. Sometimes I saw myself lying there from above, then I'd be back in the limitations of my struggling body. Eventually, I thought of God. I asked myself later, how was I thinking of God? I could barely breathe, never mind answer that question, but I somehow felt that I might have a chance at survival if I got His attention and asked Him to help me. I'd heard that He could. He was my only hope. I knew I was going to die. Note, this wasn't even a thought process, but a visceral "knowing."

I vowed to God that if He could get me out of this feeling of stuck-ness, being trapped in my own being as a death-trap, I would swear off drugs forever. Again, this wasn't anything said with words, it was my heart connecting to God. A promise to God is a serious thing. How many times have we "bargained" with God, saying we'll do this or that, if He saves us from some impending doom, only to get what we asked for but then welch on our end of the deal? I had no choice. I had to ask, or risk lying in a catatonic paralysis forever, or worse. My heart sent a message, then I lay there, waiting. I don't know how long it was after my request to God, as I think I wasn't conscious. Eventually, I was able to move my fingers. I was as excited as a half-dead person could be. Now I knew I was home free. After many hours, I regained all my faculties and to this day, I have kept my promise to God, and I have never touched a drug again. I also lost all desire. He saved me then, and removed the desire, too.

Was that the spiritual awakening I had heard about in A.A.? I began attending A.A. again, despite meetings being sparse in the rural area in which I was living. I also quickly learned to never mention I was an addict, but just an alcoholic. I would be scolded by the "old timers" of A.A., that A.A. is strictly for alcoholics and "addicts don't belong in these halls." Great. Another case of not belonging. Shirley B. agreed to sponsor me—again.

I had been given an alcohol counselor, Art, through my probation officer 3 years prior to all this, while I was still drinking and insisting "I can handle it." I decided to call Art, the counselor to whom I'd paid little attention when he would suggest perhaps drinking didn't enhance the quality of my life, and I finally agreed to "work the program." Many of us in A.A. feel "different" and like we don't belong. But, when we are with our own, we do kind of belong, at least more so than anywhere else. I saw Art weekly, even though he was an hour's drive away. I stayed sober, going to meetings, working the 12-steps of AA, for 2 out of my 4 sober years.

It was during this time, at 23, that I "found the God of my understanding" in A.A., and this "God" was a far cry from the One True God, but for the time this understanding of God worked and I began developing a relationship with Him. I spoke with Him and began to feel some closeness with Him, but it would be short-lived.

Somehow after a couple years, life got in the way and I had stopped going to meetings, was working in the nightclub business, singing and playing in bands, and I began losing touch with A.A. and with God. I spoke with God much less and sometimes completely forgot about Him. I ran the experiments. You know, the ones where we say, "oh, I can have just one drink." This experiment would be run in a multitude of fashions, most always resulting in the same drunk, blacked-out state, and me saying, "well, ok, so next time I'll try it THIS way."

No experiment yielded my intended result, and before I truly understood it, I was off and running with another three years of drunken debauchery which led me down even worse paths than my first encounter with alcoholism, and almost worse than my foray into the delusion of drugs. In my intoxicated fugue, I had drunk myself into homelessness, living like a fugitive, sleeping in the woods, an abandoned ranger station, or a farmhouse that had burned beyond usability, yet still provided partial shelter in the rain. Or I'd wake up in some strange place with unknown people and do it all again the next day. Yup. No one who goes out, i.e., relapses, ever comes back saying things got better.

Working in the music business was the perfect setup for winding up in some sketchy places with other hopeless drunks and addicts. I wasn't ever afraid, however, because I knew a long time before then, that I was exactly the person some of these well-intentioned drunks' parents had warned them about. I had lost everything: my dignity, my ability to live like a normal person, and most importantly, I had lost my relationship with God. He was so distant; I eventually never even gave Him a thought. I had managed to break every one of God's commandments at least once, and some hundreds of times. Worst of all, I was a sex addict, never realizing that this addiction was just as strong, if not stronger than the others, due to its insidiousness. I wouldn't realize this addiction for many years.

I always saw myself as a victim, suffering under male oppression most of my life. What I didn't understand or realize is, I had turned it around and as a kid, I attracted to me all the chaos and drama of illicit and sometimes perverse promiscuity. It would take a miracle and decades for me to recognize, and a few more years to leave the wretched Midian, that place where Moses voluntarily exiled himself after killing an Egyptian (Exodus 2:15). A man actually accused me of being a sexual predator, and at first I thought this was absurd. It angered me. But several years later, deep in contemplation about my life, I realized he was absolutely correct. I was horrified when I finally acknowledged it. Then I became furious at myself. I saw where I placed this before almost all other things in my life, like any addiction. Unfortunately, I wouldn't reckon this so until much later in my life.

By 1984, after having hit my lowest point in my relatively short life, I got sober again, became domiciled, (not homeless anymore), attended A.A., and asked God to remove my character defects. This time, it actually stuck. Sometimes I'd curl up with the Big Book. If you are not a "friend of Bill W.," the Big Book is A.A.'s "bible." It's the book written by Bill W. and Dr. Bob in 1939 all about the A.A. 12-steps and includes many stories of alcoholics and how A.A. works. I'd just read it for hours. I also went to meetings, worked through the 12 steps of A.A. with my A.A. sponsor, even though I am not sure I totally understood all of it. I had God back in my life to some degree, just not anywhere near what the full potential was for a God-driven life, or even close to where I'd been before. I was filled with self-loathing, shame, and guilt from collateral damage I had incurred over my drunken and addicted years, which were more accumulated years than I had ever had sober.

I would feel overwhelmed sometimes, trying to do damage control during what I assumed to be this second half of my life. I incurred a lot of damage in the first half—the fallout from many destroyed love affairs and relationships, and self-inflicted destruction from physical, mental, and emotional abuse and a couple minor legal issues. Some of this abuse was just a continuation from traveling the same frequency I had traveled in childhood, which I had come to realize was rife with abuse and neglect. I can't blame anyone, it was just what people knew to do and had probably been passed through the generations. Living in that frequency, we often attract those same experiences to ourselves as adults. Speaking of adults, having become an alcoholic at such an early age, I would have to begin again in the maturing process, picking up where I had left off—around age 10. One positive take away from this part of my life, as a songwriter and musician, it made for some of my best songwriting. What drunk in a bar doesn't love a tortured, lovesick ballad or blues?

Recovery for me was touch and go the second time at 30 years old. I had tasted the notion of God, although not really the love of God; then I lost all of it, or so it felt. Here again, I had a foot in two worlds: the world of the Prince of the World, i.e., Satan and the other in the Kingdom of God. I managed to stay sober but this time it was work, especially for the first two years. The first time I was under "the pink cloud," as they call it in A.A., filled with fresh bliss. Never would I have such innocence around recovery again. It wouldn't be until I was about 40 years old that I felt fairly comfortable in my own skin and could function in the "real world," having put my musician life aside. In my 30's, I finally attended college, which I never had done before, graduated with honors and a nursing degree and became a regular productive human with a "real day job" as a RN. I was single, after a seven-year off and on relationship, and had two beautiful daughters; the loves of my life.

I never quite saw myself as a Florence Nightingale, as nursing wasn't my first choice, but it took the least amount of schooling (or so I thought) and with the best salary for the time spent in school, as I had kids to support. But it turned out to be a fairly good choice. I truly love people, so it suited me. I carried out my duties, but I just didn't feel like I belonged anywhere. I began to think that probably I never would, and I should just get over it.

I would occasionally attend an A.A. meeting when the girls were with their father, but most of the time I was not especially involved in A.A. anymore. Something was lacking. I was most clearly involved in nature, which was my sanctuary, my higher power. Swimming in ponds, frolicking in marshes or woods brought me a peace that nothing else could provide. Nature was my church, and I was clean and sober.

Sobriety and recovery are two different things. Sobriety is abstinence from alcohol/drugs and living clean. Recovery is truly embracing our higher power and incorporating the spiritual into every moment of our lives, while passing on the beauty of service by helping other addicts and alcoholics get clean and sober. Sobriety was mine, but true recovery would elude me for quite a few more years. There was always a subtle, unconscious, soul-longing that would finally be assuaged decades later. I could have never guessed how or when that would unfold.

Chapter 13

Born Again

IT OCCURRED TO ME that I had wandered in the wilderness for almost 40 years, void of course and always questioning. I had married in the Church, then didn't attend. I was on the right path, but then we divorced and I returned to the "sexual freedom" of my teens that I had thought I'd "forfeited" when I connected with God at age 23 and got married. After conveniently "forgetting about God," and embarking upon my desert dance with the devil, I later had two abortions: one voluntary, the other coerced. The first one, I was a hopeless, homeless drunk and addict; the second, was forced by the father. Later, once sober and clean, I had two children out of wedlock, put myself through college and after eight years of school, earned a title and career. This is what I had made of my life from age 20 to 50. Forty years of wandering in a lonely abyss, doing whatever I pleased and thinking it was "fun" or even good, or right in some way. I earned a master's and a post-master's degree while often working two jobs. I was well-thought of at the hospital throughout my tenure there and for over a decade I taught in the nursing program at the local college. I would never have been able to do this drunk and addicted, but I also valued my achievements far too much.

Now I was called to go back to my own El Bethel, to the time and place where I had last known God. Where God had heard me, and I heard God! He had communicated with me, and though I wrestled with Him for those 40 years, I prayed now that God had not hardened His heart toward me and would accept me back in my incredibly fallen state. Would He? Could He? Through prevenient grace, I knew He could. I needed separation from sin and fellowship with God. With God, all things are possible!!! But the missing link here, I discovered, was Jesus. The meaning of Jesus had eluded me for so many years. I would occasionally meet a born-again Christian and while I was fascinated by their fervor and enthusiasm for The Lord, they seemed fanatical. I wasn't making sense of the source of their joy. Occasionally I'd use that phrase "What would Jesus do?" and try to act like He would, but I didn't know Him so I couldn't follow through. The key is, I didn't have a relationship with Jesus. I had the cart before the horse.

When I felt euphoric and ecstatic as I walked out of Calvary Chapel that day, as if walking on clouds, I finally understood it! Jesus and the Holy Spirit were the missing link–The Trinity! Yes! I saw Jesus finally with eyes that could see, like a veil had been lifted. He is my one and only Savior. I can't remember when I'd felt this happy!!! All my doubts had ceased. Even when Red and I would sit and I'd hear his messages and often be full of electrical tingling sensations, THIS was even bigger: SO much more intense! From 50 watts to 10,000 watts! I began to suspect Red was an integral part in building me up for *this* moment! This was a moment of true encounter and of utmost transformation.

Finally, I belonged! I belonged to a Christian community and wherever I might roam on this earth, there would be a community where I would finally feel a part.

Now, perhaps I had some people who could help me with my questions about my mysterious red dragonfly encounter. Speaking with people who were born again Christians and also to a pastor at church, I naively told my story of Red Dragon. Right off, there were red flags for the Christian community, as the Red Dragon is none other than Satan himself in the Book of Revelation. Once I found this out, I was horrified. I'd never read Revelation, thus I had never heard of THIS Red Dragon. Why had I "innocently" come up with this name for my beautiful spiritual friend that was also the name of the most notorious, nefarious creature known to God and man, and in the Bible no less. How could MY Red Dragon, my beautiful little red dragonfly, be the devil!? What kind of lesson is *that?*

Indeed, the lesson of Red Dragon eluded me more than ever. Was it all a lie? Why did I name this the "lesson" when I am more clueless than ever as to the *lesson?* The pastor warned me that often Satan can appear as a being of light. Deeply troubled by this, I consulted with a long-time born-again friend who was saved over 30 years ago. I told him the story. He focused on the "magic" aspect, and how magic is a dangerous entity in itself, the work of the devil, per scripture. He also was curious about the red dragonfly, and didn't see anything especially specious. He also took special interest in what the red dragonfly's message was to me. After pondering awhile and asking me some questions, he concluded that he felt that the enemy would not be bearing messages of hope, faith, and love. Or, if he did, it would eventually turn to the dark side. The red dragonfly never strayed from his core message of finding life's true meaning, joy, and my passionate purpose of magical blessings in my life and in every minute of every day, then, passing these blessings of faith, hope, and love forward to others. Honestly, I just didn't know what to make of any of it.

Lesson of Red Dragon

Even though I hadn't thought about Jesus too much, I was thinking of Him all the time now. I began to think about my dragonfly encounters and after contemplating the meaning for weeks, I finally decided to return to the internet and the Google Gurus to see what else I could find. I wanted to try and grasp the why of Red Dragon, the ubiquitous lesson, and whether there could be a less malevolent meaning. The following chapter is what was revealed.

Chapter 14

Research Revisited: Dragonfly & The Red Dragon

THE ANGLO-SAXON WORD FOR Dragon comes from the Greek and means "to see" or, "clear seer." This implies that the Celts considered dragons as prophets and true seers with great wisdom and clarity. To the Druids, dragons represented vitality, the psychic self, ancient wisdom, and the power of creation. Stories of dragons protecting the secret and sacred entryways to other realms are common in Celtic and Druid folklore. The "dragon spirit" is drawn to people of intellect, dignity, contagious enthusiasm, and authority. Dragons guide such individuals toward brilliance and indeed, enlightenment.[18]

The dragon is the principle of clear seeing: the ability to see things in a new light as they really are, beyond all illusions. For this reason, the dragon has great wisdom and power in myths. The wisdom of the dragon is symbolized by the treasure it guards or the pearl that the dragon carries in his mouth. To find this wisdom and knowledge, man must search in his/her inner aspects and in the unknown.[19]

Interestingly, there's a Red Dragon on the flag of Wales. The motto roughly translates as 'the Red Dragon leads us.' Unlike many European tales, dragons have strong benevolent tendencies, only harming when evil rears its ugly head.

In Revelation 12 we are introduced to the sign of a "Great Red Dragon." It is prophesied that this dragon will appear on earth with all his magnificence and power. If one is not prepared to handle this, their chances of withstanding the Dragon are none. There is no question, in Revelation the Red Dragon is Satan.

The dragonfly is generally associated with the symbolic meaning of light, change, transformation, adaptability, joy, and lightness of being, a symbol of the realm of emotions, an invitation to dive deeper into your feelings, a connection with nature's spirits, and fairies' realms. To this day, according to multiple internet sources, the dragonfly is considered to be an agent of change and presumably symbolic of a sense of self-realization and transformation. The dragonfly uses its power to control its movements so elegantly. "The eyes of the dragonfly symbolize the uninhibited vision of the mind and the ability to see beyond the limitations of the human self (360-degree vision). Dragonflies can be a symbol of self that comes with maturity. They can symbolize going past self-created illusions that limit our growth and ability to change. The dragonfly means hope, change, and love."[20]

In brief, I had found somewhat the same characteristics I'd found in my first research a few years earlier: wisdom, leadership, light, transformation, hope, emotions, magic, and love. Add to that "the ability to see beyond the limitations of the human self" And it was all coming together. Somehow, I'd managed to do that all my life! Also, "a symbol of self that comes with maturity…going past self-created illusions that limit our growth and ability to change" stood out to me. I'd lived a life of illusion, limitation, and immaturity from which I was rapidly emerging. There was nothing too dangerous or terrible, other than the obvious, the elephant in the living room: The Great Red Dragon of the Book of Revelation!

What I did notice in my research was that the dragonfly, and dragons, were more about self, self-realization, natural elements, nature, and emotions. There's wisdom and light (enlightenment), with a sort of visionary component, coupled with adaptability, change, and transformation, but focused all around self. This brought me back to the idea of Red Dragon being an Ambassador of Change. But maybe he was not the be all and end all–at ALL. Maybe he was just the beginning of a *revelation*. What if he was the catalyst that led to the change, just as the "Great Red Dragon" might be a catalyst in the Book of Revelation, mythologically giving man the knowledge of evil and the force to reach divinity?

Revelation 12:7-9 says, "Then war broke out in heaven. Michael and his angels fought against the dragon, and the dragon and his angels fought back. But he was not strong enough, and they lost their place in heaven. The great dragon was hurled down–that ancient serpent called the devil, or Satan, who leads the whole world astray. He was hurled to the earth, and his angels with him" (NIV).

In Revelation, while the dragon promotes self-ascension, the Lamb humbly steps down from the top to serve His people. I noticed red dragonfly's message to me was always focused on me first; my *self*. My self-actualization, *my* purpose, and *my* ascension were the focus even though it would be spread to others afterwards. While the message always ended up as service to others, it began with *me*. Perhaps he felt that I needed to develop *me* first before I could reach out beyond myself. Or maybe I was truly just a "lover of self." Oh man…

Chapter 15

A Hard Path to Glory

AFTER ANDY DIVORCED HIS wife, we managed to live together for close to a year, but I always harbored a feeling that a relationship conceived in dishonesty and adultery would be mired in turmoil and tragedy. Over those months of trying to find comfort and peace with one another, the opposite occurred. Andy drank heavily and was irritable, angry, verbally abusive, and resentful. His son refused to speak to him, which disturbed him immensely. There seemed to be no peace for Andy, and he lost his entire family support. He also was losing me, as I desperately tried to devise a plan to end our living arrangement without leaving him homeless.

One evening my daughter, Catie, who was a severe alcoholic, but who had been sober for five or six months, came to visit. Andy went on a drunken tirade, perhaps out of jealousy that I was spending time with someone besides him, I'm not even sure, but eventually things culminated in his assaulting both me and then, Catie. I will forever regret my daughter being subjected to this. Thankfully, Catie restrained Andy while I was still seeing stars, then talked him down until police arrived. I had called them prior to the violence that exploded in our living room, having anticipated it. Andy was arrested and taken to jail. I no longer had to figure out how to end the relationship, and I felt a great sense of relief. He had been building up to an intoxicated crescendo for a few weeks, possibly as a result of all that had gone on before with his divorce, or he was just an alcoholic in a black-out, but somehow I had a feeling that this night was going to be his cataclysmic swan song.

I took out a restraining order against Andy so he couldn't return. He had to attend A.A. and batterer's classes while living in motels until he found a more permanent place to stay. We remained separated due to his drastic increase in drinking and intolerable behavior. Some months later, he quit drinking and joined AA. After six months or so, we were back on speaking terms, and by one year, after I lifted my year-long restraining order, we were visiting with each other every once in a while, going for hikes in the woods, essentially enjoying some of our old pastimes but without any romantic involvement. For me, the romance was over. For him, there was still hope.

On his motorcycle one day in June 2019, he was riding along a winding road on the South Shore of Massachusetts and a 93-year-old driver pulled out, not looking or seeing Andy, and collided with him sending Andy flying. This nearly fatal accident left him with serious injuries; C-1 burst fracture, many other broken bones, and a sizable gash to his head that cracked his helmet in half. These multiple physical injuries and cognitive deficits, including a traumatic brain injury, changed him forever. He physically healed gradually and slowly, although he was not the same person he was. He questioned why such a terrible complex of physical and mental injuries had to occur, and his rehabilitation was grueling. He felt the tragedy of his plight; he couldn't work, had little money, even less hope, and overall was extremely depressed, and at times suicidal.

I had a feeling as to what might inspire him with an urge to press on. I had been telling him all about my experiences with God, Jesus, and the Holy Spirit. He listened with interest. One day I brought him to Calvary Chapel, briefing him on what it meant to give himself over to The Lord. He had remembered the exuberance with which I had contacted him the day I got saved. He told me he wanted to do this because he admitted he was miserable. At the end of the service, he answered an altar call and was saved. He had seen the change in me and wanted what I had. He was baptized in the Holy Spirit, and he commenced to read the entire Bible and attended church when he could. He still has multiple disabilities and angry outbursts due to his brain injury, which has alienated everyone he knew. God tore him down, pulled him apart, and ripped away from him everything he held dear, including his own physical abilities. Doctors were amazed he wasn't a quadriplegic, just as I was based on the scope of his injuries, but God had other designs.

Andy awaited a settlement from the accident for two-and-a-half years, all which was delayed due to world circumstances, such as COVID-19. It was hard to say what would become of him in his diminished state, with intellectual challenges, emotional disinhibitions, and decreased physical functioning. Andy had little to look forward to. Finally, he was awarded a settlement, but nowhere near what he had hoped. He admitted it wouldn't make up for all he had lost. I felt incredibly sad for him. Sometimes I would wonder what our relationship was all about. Why? What for? Had he stayed with his stodgy wife and comfortable home, things would be so much more tolerable—boring, but tolerable. And of course, predictable.

However, I knew from the start that if he left, he would be forever changed. I absolutely never saw *this* change coming though! And what did it mean for me? I had little to lose, yet I too was changed forever by knowing him. I often thought he may well be the last man I ever get involved with. Marriage to me seemed like nothing more than a fairytale and I was pretty sure that ship had sailed long ago. I figured he must have his own righteous path to walk, which I hoped he would find one day. I still believed God would have some path to glory for him. But what became of God's plan and of Andy is something I surely could have never imagined.

Chapter 16

A Multi-Faceted Revelation

Humble souls don't look for power in the world, but they find joy in service to others. They're satisfied, even joyous, in wisdom for wisdom's sake, not in material, superficial illusions and desires. Once we relinquish pride, then humility can take hold.

Humility is a precursor to wisdom. I had come to understand this over the past several years, but I hadn't taken measures to live this insight. While I wanted to, I simply didn't know how to do it. Having lived horizontally for so long, I longed to understand and live the vertical path to God. I was about to find out that reaching for Holy Power is letting go of our own. Our "power" is nothing more than our ego, which I had been afraid to release, because its prime directive had been to protect me all those years, and it had done a spectacular job. But now I didn't need its protection anymore, living under grace and under His blood. When fear stops frightening us, it can't stay. I had come to the place where I knew I would abide in Christ, in the Holy Spirit, and in God's Will without fear; and let go of the steering wheel. I was finally free from earthly desire and ready for Christ to take over. I came to see my responsibility was just my response to His ability and it was a gift. I welcomed being a disciple and servant. Wow.

There is a place we are each to fill and no one else can fill that place; there is something we are to do, which no one else can do. God always has the first move, but He seldom moves unless we initially ask. "you do not have because you do not ask" (James 4:2b NKJV). Lately I had been asking, and the answer would soon be revealed, and it wasn't what I expected.

One day after work, I received a notice in the mail from the Board of Registration. They were asking me to surrender my license for 30 days, in relation to that complaint I'd had lodged against me by the nursing supervisor and over which I'd lost my hospital job a couple years earlier. My heart dropped down to my stomach. I never saw this coming, but I did know in my heart of hearts, that the decision I made to skip those patients that day would come back somehow, and it had—with a vengeance. How could I forfeit my nursing license? What would this mean? What and who would I be?

I panicked.

OK. It's just 30 days, I rationalized. After the initial horror of this new reality, I began to slowly understand. I had to shed the old skin of my ego, my prestigious job, and my title. All the times I held myself above RNs ("Regular Nurses," I'd say) because I was more educated and had a "higher rank," if you will. I was boastful and arrogant at times. I hid behind the letters after my name. I flaunted my high income to others, especially men, sometimes thinking I would impress them. What a fool! I would lose my license for 30 days, and then when I got it back, I'd work on probation for one year. I was dumbfounded and humiliated. If I wouldn't see what the Lord was putting forth, the issue would have to be forced. When God plays, He plays for keeps. This was one such example, as I would've kept hanging on at my hospital job long after I'd heard God's call; and well beyond when I should have left.

Interestingly, what bothered me most was not the temporary loss of license but working on probation for a year. And it wasn't even the probation part to which I felt a visceral resistance, it was working as a NP for a whole year. I realized I didn't want to have to be a NP at all. Oddly, it is like I had shed that job, I just had not released the identity. Even though I could conceivably get my license back in 30 days after jumping through a few hoops, something unforeseen occurred that set the hoops on fire: The challenge of

COVID-19, i.e., SARS-CoV-2. My 30-day license surrender occurred in early February 2020, and we went into lockdown a couple weeks later. All state and federal agencies essentially closed to ordinary business. I couldn't get in touch with the Board, or colleagues who may be able to help; the world stood still.

I certainly had time to think. Although I could listen to patient's stories and give them compassion and heartfelt feedback, especially around their recovery, the actual prescribing of medications, especially psychotropics, which was 90% of my job, seemed misguided. Most addicts don't necessarily need antidepressants or mood stabilizers. For the most part, they need a spiritual awakening. They need a higher power. They need God. We all do. We need God to tear us apart so He can build us anew. Wasn't that what He was doing with me right now?

I certainly understood that God had to break me down in order to make me pliable in His hands. Initially, I got caught up by a beautiful, scintillating light-being, a golden filigree-winged, jewel-red dragonfly. Because, chances were, I wouldn't have paid much attention if he were a dung beetle. I thought of the Lamb in Revelation; although His lamb-like way seems to be weak and ineffective, yet His ministry is strong and eternal; the Lion of Judah. But what of the red dragonfly? Was this a ministry? Or was it a ruse?

Revelation is popular among some believers because the human brain is fascinated by the future and by prophesy, so events pertaining to "what is to come," and Eschatology are equally captivating. It's the human fallen nature to be interested in divination, oracles, and futuristic prediction. This is what keeps psychics in business. Everyone wants to hear about themselves. But what if Revelation is actually a spiritual image of our present existence with Christ? Growing in Christ, the spiritual depths of our current life pale in relation to the eternal one awaiting us. Revelation, then, isn't about the end, it's about the beginning! It is the Revelation of Jesus Christ! It's where we begin our heavenly, eternal life!

Revelation is germane to our lives and times and to every generation. God is opening His Word to hungry souls seeking the truth. If you were taught something different about Revelation, which I imagine you may have been, I understand. I was taught nothing, so fortunately I'm a clean slate. That said, when I met the red dragonfly, a.k.a., Red Dragon, I had not read the Book of Revelation. My little nickname for him, "Red Dragon," came to me from, well, I'm not sure where. Was it the Holy Spirit's sense of humor?

The Book of Daniel spoke to me in a most profound way; differently from the Book of Revelation. I just can't say enough about Daniel, the Godly, faithful man who never compromised, who taught me that my life was all about compromise and not in a good way. I bent rules, I "gave in" to temptations easily, and I believed in "white lies," which are all ungodly compromises that separate us from God. Daniel was, still is, and will always be my hero. He came to me in the Book of Daniel at a time when I needed his wisdom. His prophecies alone are enough to make a believer out of the greatest skeptic. I am forever indebted to Daniel's lessons. He was key in changing my behaviors and re-setting my priorities. He taught me honesty, integrity, and obedience to God. How I wished I'd learned this sooner.

I also reflected on who Jesus Christ was to humanity, and to me. He died for our sins. In His death, I also died. Christ, the propitiation for our sins, was our Savior. Where the disobedience of one man, Adam, had doomed humanity to eternal sin, the obedience of this one man, Jesus, redeemed us and restored us to righteousness, as long as we accepted, believed, and repented. Where Jesus delivered us from our sins, the Cross delivered us from our sinful nature. Jesus saved us from what we did, and His death on the Cross saved us from what we are. I was a sinner through and through.

Emerging from my fugue of confusion, I was walking along the beach, and I began listening to my own voice reminding me of some parts of scripture and my understanding of it around being in this world but not OF it. It began to occur to me that the whole world system, with its rulers, kings, corporations, money, political power, is all under Satan, the ruler of the world, the Prince of the Power of the Air and all that is in it. No question, we are a fallen people– Adam's rebellious children. We ARE the fallen nature of this world and Satan accesses us through our transgressions, our lack of faith, our unbelief, and mostly through our own compromise. If we are addicts and/or alcoholics, Satan sinks his hooks into us in a most insidious, excruciating, and nefarious way. This is *his* magic, if you will. Satan *is* in charge of the fallen, just as he is ruler of his fallen angels, and of us. He masters us, and we are enslaved. Until we're not! Wasn't the red dragonfly indicating that humanity needed to change? Didn't the change need to start with me?

During my time of license surrender, despite COVID, there still were colleagues I could have accessed to write letters for me espousing my professional expertise, integrity, and ability; these things would have been extremely helpful. Yet, it is as if I had blinders on. I completely didn't recognize the utilization of this, or any other avenue. I didn't have any compulsion to strategize or to scrimmage with the regulatory powers-that-be to redeem my license. Looking back, I recognize now that we will not fight for that which we do not love.

I had to lose my ego, my carnal nature of the flesh, and also lose the professional title, the name tag, the passcodes, the entry keys, the badge, the prestigious job, and the pride that went along with letters after my name. And, I had to lose the hospital. When we don't surrender when it's time for us to surrender, God will simply take it away.

Many people thought I was a doctor, and they'd call me "Doc." As an NP, we wear the white coat and do so much of the same things as doctors, and I relished those things many times when people thought this, so I usually didn't correct them. In my heart of hearts, I understood that had I grown up in a different class and culture, I could have easily become a doctor. I was prohibited by my old-world upbringing that told lower-class girls that their only hope at success was to be married. After all, I was so much more than "just a nurse." I was all that!

Sometimes I'd catch a slim notion that I had to stop seeing myself as better than; better than the blue-collar worker, the housekeepers, the "Andy's" of the world who labored outdoors because all I was doing was covering up the vacuous void of futility and insincerity within me, that gnawing feeling of not ever being good enough and never belonging. Part of my becoming a NP in the first place was because I had something to prove. People would respect me then. They would be impressed, and my mother, who had marginally tolerated me and my lifestyle, actually showed me admiration and honor once I became a RN. I was so unused to this. She seemed, for once, proud of me. So, why not optimize all this and become a NP? Sadly, once I did she was beyond proud of me—for the first and only time in my life, she actually bragged about me. Imagine that!

I finally realized over time that I had to learn to love myself. I had to have love and respect for me; for what I am, not for what I do. I needed to stop trying to impress the world and start to remove myself *from* the world. Perhaps finding love for myself was where Red Dragon came in. He chose ME. I was chosen and I was so incredibly unused to that. I was so used to being less-than, put aside, second or third-best, or just nothing at all.

Over time and more transformation, I found self-respect, dignity, and true love for who, not what I am. With this, I could go forth to truly and unconditionally love and serve others, finally finding what I'd ultimately give away. I started out in life drinking at seven years old. I never developed myself like most people do, being intoxicated so much while still in the single digits. I had to start from the single digits of childhood and learn maturity as an adult. Yes, the "Red Dragon" taught me love of self! I saw that I'd spent much of my adult life with the brain of a kid. "Men will be lovers of themselves, lovers of money, boastful, proud, abusive......"(2 Tim. 3.2) Because I had no self-worth, I at least had to develop a sense of self, which I was finally able to do. Timothy meant that this sort of love of self was negative, as some love of self is, yet I believe, some self-love is necessary in order to love others. We can't give from an empty well. It's the second part of the Great Commandment: "And he said to him, 'You shall love the Lord your God with all your heart and with all your soul and with all your mind. This is the great and first commandment. And a second is like it: You shall love your neighbor as yourself'" (Matt. 22:37-39). I count it as joy—JOY: J = Jesus, O = Others, Y = You.

I already had the money, the boastfulness, and the pride. I realized it had to be discarded, which was when I jettisoned by job and my career, or it jettisoned me. The dilemma presented to me was, what and who am I now that I'm not a NP? It felt like I had lost my "self," my status, my individuality. Was NP what I am? Or what I do? I had become so engulfed in my ego-identification, I lost who *I* was. *Me*.

Paradoxically, I had to once again gain a sense of myself, so I could lose myself, so I could relinquish myself and my ego to the extent of total humility and humble servitude to others and to causes far greater than I. I had to find me, again, so I could give myself away. The void within me became the God-shaped space that only God and His Holy Spirit, through Jesus Christ could fill. No man or career ever could. This ministry and mission were to create more love in the world. Jesus's Love. God's Love. Spread the Good News.

This may not compute for many people who learned the meaning of the Book of Revelation in some particular way, especially for those who learned it literally and concretely. To extrapolate out to my life, an understanding of an abstract interpretation of Revelation might even be considered blasphemous to some. So be it. I am giving you what I have. Please feel free to prove me wrong, but remember, I doubt that anyone except Jesus has the final answer on the meaning of the Book of Revelation of Jesus Christ. At the risk of oversimplification, Revelation is a glance into intense spiritual warfare where good battles against evil. God the Father and Jesus Christ oppose Satan and his demons. Jesus already won the war, but in the end, He will come again to the earth and everyone will know he is the King and Lord of the Universe. God and His people win.

Even though my story and this lesson didn't turn out like I expected, the message and lesson of the red dragonfly was still in keeping with who I have become and with the Great Commission. With every person we touch, our love grows larger, grander, brighter, and stronger, filling that emptiness, the God-shaped space within us. Then, spreading the Gospel of Jesus Christ. What if I lead by example? What if I bear witness to testify to people that they can have love in their lives too, just like I have in mine? God's love, saved by Jesus and the Holy Spirit. What a testimony! And this time, unlike my coaching foray, it's real!

I envision harmonious relationships with all living things as part of our understanding of God's Kingdom on Earth. This can be seen in the prophecies of Isaiah, for example: "The wolf shall lie down with the lamb, the leopard shall lie down with the kid, the calf and the lion and the fatling together, and a little child shall lead them .... They will not hurt or destroy on all my holy mountain; for the earth will be full of the knowledge of the Lord as the waters cover the sea." (Isa.1:6, 9 NRSV). We truly *can* have heaven on earth with the peace of God.

Chapter 17

Testing the Spirits

As a Christian, I accepted the teaching that we should "test the spirits to see whether they are from God" (1 John 4:1). How would I test the red dragonfly? Or better yet, this story? After having been saved, and still visiting with red dragonfly, I began to wonder how I would discern whether the Holy Spirit had used red dragonfly as a messenger, or whether he was of malevolent origins? I had to ask of course, why any less-than-divine entity would prepare me for Jesus?

So how *did* red dragonfly react to the notion of Jesus? Was this even testable?

I tried this test to the best of my ability, literally asking him, and I saw no adverse reaction from him. He seemed impartial. While this may not be definitive, never did Red prompt or provoke negativity, nor did I ever feel any attempt from him to dominate me in any way or steer me in an unfavorable direction. He didn't flee at the mention of Jesus Christ. What he provided was a framework for what I thought of initially as intentional spiritual work. It did seem important to me was that he, spontaneously over time, was preparing me for my encounter with Jesus. Also, he focused me on the positive energy of helping and servitude and taking the next step in becoming less "of this world."

Could my relationship with Red have been considered idolatry? An idol is any created thing that is given the place of highest honor in our hearts, the place that rightly belongs to God alone. Christianity might say the danger of such a thing as Red is nothing short of idolatry, which leads us to stop listening to God. We turn away from Him and turn toward the idol. In my case, I had abandoned any notion of God decades earlier, so there was no turning away from Him. Red was, over time, actually leading me closer to Him. Over the years of getting to know Red, I had to somehow assign a source from which he would have come. I began referring to it as "The All That Is," or, "The Universe," since "God" had long ago left my lexicon. This was as close to naming the Creator as I could get. Earlier in my substance use recovery, my higher power was just that: "My Higher Power." I knew there was "something greater than me," and sometimes I called it God, but I had no understanding. God was a word. And the possibility that Red symbolized the Holy Spirit surely never crossed my mind. I had no idea even who the Holy Spirit was.

Christ says that perfect love casts out fear. In dealing with messages from the natural world, or from its creatures, loving acceptance of all aspects of reality is crucial. Fear only magnifies a perceived threat, which in this case would be a little being of nature. When God created animals, he declared their creation to be "good" (Gen. 1:25.) God can work through animals; the Bible says, "God commanded ravens to bring Elijah food while he was there, [by the brook] and they did" (1 Kings 17:4-6). The Bible mentions sparrows, doves, and all manner of creatures.

Now, as for Red being the enemy, that false "being of Light" that we read of in the Bible, aren't they malevolent spirits which feed off human desperation? Yes, they may be alluring and seductive at first, but don't they always eventually degrade themselves and their victims into a sinful state? I was almost thoroughly broken when I encountered Red, way more so than I knew. I definitely had a certain type of subconscious remoteness, an incompleteness even, which explains why I was attracted to Andy. I just didn't realize it then. I thought I was in a fairly pleasant state of mind, even if blissfully ignorant to my actual state of mind. At the core of my being, however, I was begging to be ripped open, exposed, and made vulnerable. My pride and hubris were tremendous, but my humility was in the toilet.

A sinner all my life, I was in a sinful state long before Red arrived on the scene. I was definitely undergoing a period of transition, with no map, GPS, or plan. Change was in the air, so I did have some mild uneasiness around what I perceived was to be a major life transition. At one point, I even wondered if I was being prepared for death. Yet unafraid, I forged ahead. Looking back, I *was* being prepared for death! It wasn't physical death but dying so that I could be born again! I began wondering if powerful communicators like the red dragonfly were guides, messengers, like angels leading us toward a path of righteousness, not down a twisted road to ruin.

But Red Dragon Magic? Was this the concept upon which I was building my ministry? Well, actually yes. What began as a seemingly "shamanic" experience slowly evolved into a new walk, a different path, and a love for our Lord and Savior. Talk about having a foot in two worlds! As I walk in the light of Jesus, I DO have a foot in two worlds: one foot on earth and one foot in Heaven. Yet, the two worlds are really one. This is something of myself that I give to the world, the blending of these seemingly different approaches. I will never be that woman who grew up in the church, had pastors for parents and lived a righteous life. I came from the dark side, the spiritual "other side of the tracks," a mercenary and tainted past; just the type who Jesus came to minister to. I was performing a delicate balancing act, wanting spirituality but coming up empty. There are plenty of people like this who think they're love and light, but once they catch a glimpse of the One True Love and Light, their counterfeit pales in comparison. I have lived it, so I can share with you what I have found.

The Red Dragon does symbolize Satan in the Book of Revelation. The red dragonfly, however, seemed to have no evil agenda. He speaks to our earthly, natural experiences and desires here as humans, who, by our faith and by God's grace and mercy, are saved from ourselves. In Revelation, John uses symbolism and metaphor along with reality for the life and times of his day and of days and times to come, pertinent to each period of humanity. Why I chose the name Red Dragon is still beyond me. I wish I had a tidy, well-ordered answer, but I don't. Perhaps this is a revelation for another time.

Speaking of end times and judgments, I could imagine the judgment and persecution from all my new age friends, the disappointment in my conversion, and the sense of betrayal. I pursued my new-found love, God, with unbridled abandon, however, only one or two of my acquaintances eschewed my passion for Him. Everyone else accepted this about me with open arms, even if they weren't believers. What I came to find was surprising: some really were, and are believers, but they just didn't announce it or in some cases, admit it. There have been a couple who once they saw my joy and serenity, marveled and wanted some of what I had, and have also converted to Christ; a blessing for which I must always be careful to give God all the honor and glory. Christians don't make others Christians–God does!

My spirit-testing wasn't exactly yielding satisfactory results, particularly with this story, this experience was of God and whether it should be told to glorify Him. However, God works on His timetable, or lack thereof, not on mine. What would be revealed to me in the future would literally blow me away.

Chapter 18

The Real Ministry ~ Sober Home Living; The Affinity House

THE TIME CAME WHEN I had fulfilled my obligations in order to get my nursing license back. I acclimated to the one-year probation part but working as a NP for one whole year seemed abhorrent to me. How a career that I had embraced for so long could now be an anathema still left me bewildered. All I wanted to do was study the Holy Word, garden, ride my bike, take nature photos, volunteer, and live my ministry at what came to be known as The Affinity House. Apart from this, I was also receiving a call to ministry, pastoral ministry. I didn't answer right away, as the idea seemed just a little absurd.

People could, and can, see that the Holy Spirit is in me. They see me as changed, and for the better. No one ever said it, but I must have been kind of an asshole when I was at the height of my career. But now, I feel definite with the Infinite, and now I know who the Infinite truly is! I know my purpose and my calling ~ To give myself away, pick up my cross and follow Jesus, spreading the Gospel to glorify God.

In retrospect, I had no idea how this would show up, however, a shifting of energy was in the works six years prior to my being saved and I'd been waiting patiently in a holding pattern since March 2018 for my marching orders. I wasn't in any hurry. I'd wondered about my purpose for years. Then, everything happened as if in an instant. In the middle of December 2018, I passed papers on a home (not far from Rockland) in which my two daughters, Christine and Catie, and I opened in January 2019. "The Affinity House" is a nurturing and empowering sober home for women committed to their recovery in beautiful Nantasket Beach, in the seaside town of Hull, Massachusetts.

My daughters and I had spoken often of how we would run a sober house differently than we had seen others run, such as the one in which my daughter Catie was living in Rockland. So many people went into this business with probable good intentions at first, but somehow seemed to drift from altruistic to unethical. Some homes were run by addicts who may not have been stable in their own recovery. Stories of exploitation and drug-using abounded in many of these homes.

The whole process of looking at properties, discussing how we would run the sober house, and actually buying it was a whirlwind that spanned no more than three months! I felt like I was not only being led to do this, but that I was swirling in the vortex of a Power far greater than me, having researched relatively little into the whole venture. We named it the "Affinity House," which was a name my daughter Catie offered up, and we all liked it.

Catie was initially designated as the House Manager but still in early sobriety herself, this responsibility proved too formidable, so she stepped down. I had sold my home on Cape Cod and was living in the Hull home, The Affinity House, and became the House Manager when Catie was unable to do so. Christine, my oldest, is a financial whiz and a dedicated ally to the cause of recovery, so she has stepped up to co-manage the house. At The Affinity House I have had the opportunity to minister to women in recovery and help show them the way to a better life. In some cases, I've been able to lead them to Jesus, our Savior, the Holy Spirit and a loving God, our Father, who loved us first.

Just down the street from The Affinity House is the Anchor of Hull, a recovery center run by Kurt, a pastor at North Street Community Church of the Nazarene, a wonderful community church nearby in Hingham, which I have since joined. We all have the same objective: We guide and empower weary, broken souls ~ addicts & alcoholics in recovery, to the wholeness of God's Living Spirit, giving hope, faith, and blessings of Jesus' love! What has happened here has been a culmination of everything that has occurred since this adventure began seven years ago.

Dennis Scott, retired Pastor and father of lead Pastor, Jeremy Scott, at North Street Community Church suggested I obtain a local pastor license, which I did. I have since acquired my District license. Can ordination be far away? We hold Bible study weekly at our sober house, and we also have a lively Bible Study with the Anchor. I attend Nazarene Bible College's Ministry Preparation Program.

Chapter 19

The Long Goodbye

A S I SHARED BEFORE, Catie could no longer be house manager of The Affinity House, even though she had been initially involved and even chose the house name. She was a great manager, but she inherited my genetic predisposition for addiction, and alcohol was her drug of choice. She was an active alcoholic by summer following her high school graduation, despite having been captain of varsity cheerleading for three years, earning the title, "Captain Cate." She had also embarked on a successful career selling Cadillacs before she was even old enough to buy one. By 18 years old, she had bought her own Mitsubishi 3000GT VR4, which was a rare sports car that she had discovered and loved since she was 12 years old. She had basically manifested most of her childhood dreams by age 18, which was when her drinking spiraled out of control and the next 15 years would bring a string of bad decisions, toxic relationships, and what

I observed, even long before I myself got saved, to be demonic possession.

The girl who so often put others before herself, who was beautiful, empathic, intuitive, kind, and thoughtful had devolved into a self-absorbed, manipulative, deceitful, recalcitrant teenage-like woman whose entire life and focus was on alcohol. Multiple ER and hospital visits often resulted in fruitless detoxes, along with the occasional detox romance, and new techniques learned for alcohol acquisition. Homelessness and several violent relationships brought a plethora of concussions, broken bones, and bruises of body, mind, and spirit. Catie was no longer herself. By 33 years old, she was merely a shell, a shadow of her former self. She was incapacitated by her own delusions, which, by virtue of her tragic trajectory of alcoholism, became full-blown possession by the demons of alcohol that could literally be seen in her eyes and in her actions, by any eye trained to discern such things. Even before being filled with the Holy Spirit, I plainly saw the spirits of evil that inhabited my daughter's body and by the time Catie was 23, I sensed that this could be "the long goodbye."

I stood by and watched the horror unfold, chaos, grand mal seizures, violence, lawlessness, and neglect of self and family. She was thoroughly consumed by the demonic influence of alcohol and seemed to show no remorse or overt desire for repentance. She didn't seem to care who she took down with her on her way, and yet she claimed to do it all in the name of "helping" other people, particularly men she tried to "fix," yet in whom she didn't bring out the best. These men were almost always drug addicts who were as lost as she.

Catie would accrue several months or more of sobriety and I would initially be hopeful but, after having my heart stomped on time and again, my hope began to fade, although I've never abandoned hope. I still keep hope alive as long as Catie is still in her body. I've told her that there's nothing she can do to make me love her more and nothing she can do to make me love her less. This is the same way God loves all of us, and I know when I was at my worst, I must have broken God's heart as He is as loving a Father as ever there was, is, and always will be. Just like Hosea's heart was broken when his promiscuous wife couldn't be true to him, he never stopped loving her and he recognized his love was not unlike God's love for His fickle people. God never stops loving us, and I never stop loving Catie, my beautiful, empathic child.

My suggestions to her about opening her heart to God, to Christ, has fallen on deaf ears, yet we never know when seeds are planted. I remembered my own obstinance when people mentioned a "higher power" and I wasn't yet ready to receive it. I blamed alcohol itself at times for her addiction to it, or occasionally I'd blame her father who had abandoned her years before, but most of the time, I blamed myself. If I had only done this or not done that; so many roads that I might have traveled with her, besides the one I took—if only.

Then one day, out of nowhere, she texted me from a hospital with the cryptic phrase, "I'm pregnant." She told me she was going into a program for pregnant women because she said she truly wanted this baby. Her plan was to be alcohol-free for her nine months, which, to me, definitely would take a miracle. But then I thought, wait: This is exactly how God works! This tiny little life just could be the one thing that changes everything. I'd always prayed for Catie, but now here was the new inclusion of another soul—one who is knitted together in her womb with the potential to absolutely turn her life upside down. At this writing Catie is six months pregnant, sober and radiant! I am excited to see how this all will unfold.

Chapter 20

Bloom Where You're Planted

ONE DAY IN MAY of 2019 at The Affinity House, I was weeding around our yard thinking, "I could do this all day." I was really enjoying gardening, as I always had when I'd owned a home. Out of the blue (well, not really… there are no coincidences, just Divine Appointments), I had an idea. Why not advertise weeding and charge something like $25/hour to weed people's gardens? I had no idea if the idea would fly, but I put a free ad on Facebook and before long, I had so many jobs I raised my hourly rate from $25/hour to $35/hour, and then to $45/hour in just one month to try to "weed" out some jobs as I couldn't keep up! It was hard work, but I was outside and making people happy because their gardens went from a tangled weedy mess to an organized area of beauty. There was hardly any price people wouldn't pay for beauty. I still love making people happy.

I pondered over my years of wondering what my life purpose was, and what *was* that message from Red Dragon? It was definitely a message from The Holy Spirit, sent through a beautiful creature of nature; a being that would surely attract my attention. He was both a symbol and a being that I would feel an "affinity" for and trust. I marveled at the simplicity of His message as I moved from questioning my life's purpose to asking God what His Will was for me, now that I'd given my life over to Him?

The answer was simple enough that a child could understand. Yes, I had to laugh at myself: This truly *is* a planet for slow learners! One point of this message and its curious messenger was very clear, especially once I considered why the phrase "Bloom Where You're Planted" had been dropped into my head as if by an unknown deliverer way back when it came to me in a lucid dream. What does "Bloom Where You're Planted" even mean, anyway?

First off, it's what I named my weeding and gardening service in Hull, and who blooms where they're planted better than weeds?

But wait, there's more.

I began this business because I love gardening. I also love making people happy. And, on a more practical side, having no initial income, I had to work. When I moved to Hull from Cape Cod, I was starting over in business, having done a little landscaping with Andy on the side in my previous hometown of Yarmouth after I'd left the hospital. A lady I worked for there one day had a slew of potted plants and she gave me a little Lamb's Ear plant and she said a phrase I'd not heard before ~ "Bloom Where You're Planted." I loved it! And it stayed with me. I'd find myself saying it now and then, here and there. It rang true.

To me, this phrase can mean: Be content where God has placed you in life and make the most of your particular calling, flourishing where you can. Constantly daydreaming about having more things, or a nicer body, or a new relationship, or a new house, or anything which we don't have or have enough of, will lead to personal instability and lack of productivity. So instead, no matter where you are 'placed,' you succeed there. You were planted there for a reason, and you needn't know what that reason is ~ just bear fruit, prosper, thrive. The 'how' takes care of itself.

Incidentally, the Lamb's Ear plant came with me to Hull, where it is blooming beautifully. I have been so fortunate to have been able to bloom wherever I am planted, with reasonable, and at times remarkable success at supporting myself, finding "good" jobs and occupying space in a positive way. I have learned to bring my comfort zone with me wherever I go, perhaps because I have spent an inordinate amount of time out of my comfort zone. So, I determine to carry it with me or else spend my life unable to stand being in my own skin. Being a child of God makes the whole comfort zone issue easy.

At The Affinity House, sometimes women come with nothing. They come out of jail, detox, rehab, or off the street. I invite women to come work with me weeding to offer them the opportunity to get their hands in soil, earn an honest (and very good) wage, learn a skill and 'bloom where they're planted.' If they're good at it, I pay them the same amount I pay myself. Women who came to our home with nothing are now blooming! Some started just with modest gardening and others became quite adept at it. This is a God-given gift that I can pass on to them.

With heartfelt gratitude for God's transforming love and mercy, a major transformational shift is ushered in. Limbic music, living in passion, in meaning from the heart, in God's Will, on purpose, shedding the old "skins" and "sins," becoming new, and "being in our being-ness." With the Holy Spirit we walk with and belong to Jesus, our Savior and God, calling to all who are lost. Those we seek are also seeking us with mutual attraction. We travel the frequency of God's Magical Blessings! With Him, all things are possible! Who wouldn't want this?

The Holy Spirit leads me on my path to transcendence. This is the portal through which I've emerged to express my story through Divine Design. All the while, I am a channel through which The Spirit's Love and Blessings pour out to the world. Once we fly, we can never return to our watery underworld.

Our mission and commission is to spread Hope, Faith, Joy, Love & God's Miraculous Blessings.

Chapter 21

A New and Old Healthcare System: Temple of the Holy Spirit

ACCORDING TO THE ONLINE Etymology Dictionary (https://www.etymonline.com), holism is the theory that parts of a whole are in intimate interconnection, such that they cannot exist independently of the whole, or cannot be understood without reference to the whole, which is thus regarded as greater than the sum of its parts. I cannot think of this "holism" without also entertaining the word, "holy." While holy is perfect and flawless, holism speaks to a different perfection where the "whole" is the perfect condition or status of an organism. When we begin to separate the parts, it can become unbalanced, thus dis-ease occurs.

I asked the Spirit to breathe insight into this book in general, but especially into this chapter and the first words that came were these: The path to healthiness and to holiness is the same path. To be holy we must be separated from the ordinary, the world. It suggests that we are or become clean, versus unclean. This isn't about hygiene but about our spirit. Is our spirit clean, undefiled, and pure? Or is it fraught with contamination, demonic influence, and worldly feculence? Many of us would admit that our spirit lives somewhere in the middle. Here is an area where there can be no compromise. The Book of Daniel taught me about compromise, and we'll get to that shortly.

Having been a happy gardener for the last four years, my back now somewhat limits my gardening and landscaping activities. Congenital scoliosis with years in the making is progressing at an alarming rate. Perhaps more of God's humble pie? I always prided myself on my physical prowess and athletic abilities, as for a good part of my life I had something to prove. I thought I no longer felt this way, however, the residual repercussions of this boastful behavior had already taken hold. What was I being taught now? Did I still have something to prove after all? Had I maybe been showing off a little with my physical strength, endurance, and stamina? Were the pigeons of ego coming home to roost—again?

I've been seeing a chiropractor, had rounds of steroid and trigger point injections, physical therapy; I also tried regenerative medicine, including platelet-rich plasma and Wharton's jelly injections with some benefit, however, these won't restructure my spine. All these treatments are akin to getting a haircut when one really needs brain surgery. In my case, back surgery may be the only option left. I lean into the Lord for guidance, but for now, Andy helps with much of the work for this fourth summer in my gardening business. This makes me a little sad, but it also opens doors for others to be able to learn this delightful trade and make it their own. I must find a positive viewpoint, and this may be part of it.

Apart from my back issue, I am incredibly healthy in terms of no illness along with good organ function and overall great health. People have asked me how this is, as I take no medications for the usual ills of our day: no antihypertensives for high blood pressure, no insulin or anti-hypoglycemics for diabetes, no statins for hyperlipidemia. I don't smoke or drink. I've always been a bit underweight, probably because I'm active and have a high metabolism.

When people ask me, "how do you do it?" I respond with, "follow me around; do what I do and eat what I eat." My thoughts are if they are as active as I and eat a lot of fruit, vegetables, fish, a little dairy, breads of all kinds, no coffee, just tea; plenty of nuts, beans, popped corn; no processed foods or soda, they may fare as I do, genetics aside. Many of my food choices are made based on what I like and don't like, not on what I think is "healthy." I simply enjoy food and the food I love happens to be pretty good for us.

I think the real secret to good health, to your own personal correct weight and to a high energy level, is engaging in healthful practices; not because you feel obligated to, but because our body is truly a temple, a shrine in which the Holy Spirit dwells. "Do you not know that your bodies are temples of the Holy Spirit, who is in you, whom you have received from God? You are not your own; you were bought at a price. Therefore honor God with your bodies" (1 Cor. 6:19-20 NIV).

So, it isn't about depriving one's self of food, or trying to diet, or measuring portions; it's not going to the gym every day (unless you love doing that); but rather it is developing a taste (if you don't have it already) for unprocessed foods, plenty of fresh produce, unprocessed fish of all types and breads with olive oil, nut butter, cream cheese or butter (any of these work). Oddly, since childhood I never liked hot dogs, anything salty, deli meats, American cheese, pickles, and a few other things that as it happens, aren't especially "healthy" to eat. I can't explain it, it's just always been this way. In the realm of psychosomatic medicine, one could also say a positive attitude leads to good health. I've always been a positive person.

Aside from what we eat, we should be sure to get plenty of fresh air, spend time in nature, put our hands and feet in soil or sand often, walk or ride a bike rather than drive everywhere, practice stretching and balance daily, preferably in nature. These are only a few ideas, and ones that will come naturally once we open our body to share it with the Holy Spirit.

But wait, there's more. Here is the secret within the secret: Everything you do, incorporate the Holy Spirit. Include Him in all activities, invite Him to dine with you, walk with you, pray with you, meditate with you, swim, hike, bike with you. Take Him everywhere (which you can't help but do because He's in you), but it is your "awareness" of him that is important. Count everything as joy and have a grateful heart. He is your guide, advocate, comforter. Treat Him as such and consider His feelings. Incidentally, I use the pronoun "He" a lot, but of the Trinity, the Holy Spirit is the One member that is originally feminine. According to Strong's Concordance, the Greek for Holy Spirit is a feminine noun, πνεῦμα (pneuma), that means wind, breath. In the older Hebrew, Holy Spirit is רוּחַ (ruach), and is also a feminine noun meaning wind, spirit.

One time I was walking the beach on a sunny July day, noticing multiple couples walking the beach, some hand-in-hand. Having been single a long time, I thought how it would be nice to have someone to walk and talk with, hold hands, go to dinner with sometimes, and as I was thinking this, I felt a tingling in both of my hands. Before I had a chance to think how weird this was, I had a thought literally inserted into my mind; "take my hand." But it was both hands! Before I knew it, there I was, grinning like a fool, holding hands with Jesus on my right, and the Holy Spirit on my left. I was the happiest lady on the beach that day! Who knows what people thought as I walked along laughing, smiling, both hands slightly lifted out on both sides! And, I couldn't have cared less what anyone thought, in fact, I kind of wished I could've shared the experience with them.

Whenever you feel alone, invite the Holy Spirit to join you and see what happens. Soon you'll be inviting the Spirit at all times, lonely or happy! Whenever you open to God, Jesus, the Holy Spirit, watch and see what happens. In the show, "The Chosen," (Director Dallas Jenkins), Mary Magdalene says to Nicodemus, "I was one way… and now I am completely different. And the thing that happened in between… was Him."

> "But now thus says the LORD, he who created you, O Jacob, he who formed you, O Israel: 'Fear not, for I have redeemed you; I have called you by name, you are mine'" (Isa. 43:1 ESV).

I could write a book just on alternative healthcare practices with all my wonderful colleagues who have also taken alternative paths to true healing. You see, modern medicine treats symptoms but doesn't address root causes. There is little that is holistic in Western medicine, so many have pursued different routes to tap into the body's own wisdom of its needs for maintaining its wholeness. When I was posting about this book on social media, an outpouring of my friends in healthcare and also people I didn't even know rushed in on this conversational thread discussing the many different holistic approaches they were using instead of just allopathic, or westernized medicine. Honestly this could truly open the eyes of the medical profession, who especially recently, has not been "following the science"–*their* science–very logically, diligently, or open-mindedly. Science is meant to be questioned and this opportunity for rational discourse has been lost. Hopefully, science finds its way back to the right relationship with wisdom.

In scientific debate, sometimes compromise can be healthy. However, regarding our own bodies, our choices, and how we treat ourselves is often not up for concessions. The Book of Daniel begins in chapter 1 when Daniel and three other Hebrew boys become captives of Babylon. They are the brightest and the best and are being groomed by the king for Babylonian duty, so they receive good food and treatment, are re-named, and taught the new Babylonian language. Right off, Daniel and his three friends refuse to eat the meats and royal fare or drink the king's wine, because of strict Mosaic

Law around dietary restrictions. Amazingly, Daniel negotiates a plan with the head Eunuch, who is in charge of their food. The plan worked and the Hebrew boys remain "clean."

Daniel chapter 3 tells of how three Jews, their new Babylonian names Shadrach, Meshach, and Abednego, were thrown into a fiery furnace for their refusal to bow down to a giant statue of Babylonian King Nebuchadnezzar. The King demanded that everyone bow down to his statue or die. To the pagans, there was no question that they would bow down to it, rather than die. But Shadrach, Meshach, and Abednego spurned an offer of pardon from the King if they would change their minds and worship him. They didn't and so they were thrown into a blazing furnace, but God honored them because they honored Him and brought them out of the fire completely unharmed, to the King's utter amazement. Nebuchadnezzar responded by acknowledging that the Jews worshipped the Most High God, and he promoted Shadrach, Meshach, and Abednego in his government.

Later, in chapter 6 of Daniel, a similar situation would happen where Daniel refuses to compromise regarding the worship of his God to worship a pagan one, and he is thrown into a den of hungry lions. He too is released unscathed, and that King, Babylonian King Darius, recognizes that Daniel's God protected him, "Daniel answered, 'May the king live forever! My God sent his angel, and he shut the mouths of the lions. They have not hurt me, because I was found innocent in his sight. Nor have I ever done any wrong before you, Your Majesty'. The king was overjoyed and gave orders to lift Daniel out of the den. And when Daniel was lifted from the den, no wound was found on him, because he had trusted in his God" (Dan. 6:21-23 NIV). Throughout this Old Testament book, Daniel never compromised, but retained his faith in God and His wisdom even though Daniel was serving foreign kings in a pagan country far away from his native land of Jerusalem in Judea.

"The Spirit of truth: The world cannot accept him, because it neither sees him nor knows him. But you know him, for he lives with you and will be in you" (John 14:17 NIV). "Take the helmet of salvation and the sword of the Spirit, which is the word of God" (Eph. 6:14). The sword of the Spirit spoke to me through God's Word–the Book of Daniel. One year my entire 40-day Lenten period was spent studying this wonderful book. Had I known this sooner I would have avoided much heartache and trouble had I not compromised in so many areas of my life.

(I pray) "that the God of our Lord Jesus Christ, the Father of glory, may give you the Spirit of wisdom and of revelation in the knowledge of him" (Eph. 1:17 ESV). The Holy Spirit is the source of all wisdom and revelation about the character of God. The Holy Spirit isn't there just to give us "head knowledge", but He is in us to saturate our hearts with the knowledge of God so that we can more intimately experience Him. Now that's a relationship worth investing in!

Chapter 22

Andy, Revisited

AT TIMES, JUST WHEN we think a relationship has played itself out and we have moved on, we discover that it, and we, have not; that there is more, something was overlooked, or perhaps has evolved. From some sudden and almost forgotten place, the notion of Andy appeared in November of 2021. Actually, it was the prompting of the Holy Spirit, Who encouraged me to look him up. Andy and I always kept in touch, although not often of late, but just enough to keep track of each other. He hadn't been as responsive as usual to my texts to him, so I asked the Holy Spirit to show me why. To my surprise, The Spirit indicated to me that Andy had a girlfriend that he wasn't telling me about. When I mentioned it to him, he admitted he did, and he'd gotten into the relationship deeper than he'd planned, whatever that meant. He also was extremely unwell.

When I suggested he and I might not be done with each other, he became dumbfounded, admitting he had a dilemma now. Andy never recovered from his traumatic brain injury so I could see navigating my emotional curve ball to him caught him off-guard which presented a different dilemma to me. How could I have a deeply meaningful relationship with a man who no longer possessed the faculty of abstraction? His thinking seemed concrete and as his post-TBI cognitive testing had revealed, he now had the intelligence of a 12-14 year-old where executive function was concerned. While I knew this, I now could see firsthand what this looked like in action. To try and describe feelings, spiritual and emotional, to him seemed beyond his understanding. Yet, it wasn't. He still understood love and feelings in simplistic terms, which to me may actually be the best way. Ascertaining his feelings for his girlfriend was challenging. He did say she also had a head injury, so they had commonalities. He appeared to be fond of her, yet he tried to minimize his involvement, complaining that she wasn't a good match, and she was "just someone to hang out with."

As you know, I've always been a loner, living on the outer periphery of relationships or more often, living alone and being content with this "nobody's wife and everybody's sweetheart" persona. Truth is, always feeling a foot in two worlds, I couldn't be fully present to a mate. I always felt that the counterfeit 'me,' the 40% that lives in this world is an avatar and the true authentic 'me,' the 60% is the one living somewhere beyond these foreign skies. Some force was drawing me to Andy and while I felt the Holy Spirit, I was also being skeptical, my overthinking mind questioning whether a darker spirit was at work.

We spent a day together, which felt like "old times." Apart from his newly-found relationship, Andy was also experiencing some serious health problems, primarily hypertension for which he was taking three antihypertensives and still having blood pressure readings that were barely compatible with life. He disclosed a less-than quality lifestyle, especially when he was with his girlfriend, who smoked heavily and "drinks a lot of beer," as he described it. I realized he was actually quite ill, hadn't been eating, was also drinking, and seemingly had lost hope about his life. The civil suit for his accident dragging on, interrupted by the Covid pandemic and his health issues, had taken their toll. In short, he was a mess. He had also backslidden in his relationship with the Lord, admitting that he didn't even pray anymore.

Despite all this, I still felt the same love for him that I'd felt over 5 years ago when we met. Why? And why now? I was leaving Massachusetts to return to Florida in a week. And he finally had a girlfriend, but he looked like he had one foot in the grave. He looked like a homeless drunk guy. Why did my interest rekindle for him at this time? If he had asked me to marry him, right then and there, I probably would have. Crazy. Was this an interference by the enemy? I felt so suddenly drawn to him, which is why I had to find out if he had someone else so I wouldn't make a fool of myself, which I did anyway, telling him I still loved him and thought we had a chance, even knowing of his new lady friend.

Seeing his struggle with this new knowledge and his being so caught up in what to do about me, about her, and about himself, I thought long and hard and decided I had made a mistake. I had no right to come barging into his life and turn it upside-down. Hadn't I done that once already? Here he had a woman with whom he could sleep with and share daily nuances of life with. Me, I was heading to Florida, where he would not be apt to go. He seemed to see his life now as a disabled person, living in disabled people's housing, dating a disabled alcoholic woman while reverting to alcohol himself, and all with absolutely no future and from what I could tell, no God. He hadn't even mentioned God during our renewed conversations unless I asked.

I told him I had made a mistake and he should carry on in his life as he was. The Spirit wouldn't let me leave him alone. If nothing else, I needed to help him with his health, or he really wouldn't be alive much longer. He had been hospitalized four times in the past month, couldn't keep any food down, felt dizzy and weak most of the time, and couldn't control his blood pressure, all within the context of drinking. Meanwhile, when I told him of my mistake, he disagreed and that very day he went and told his girlfriend he didn't want to see her anymore. He stuck to it. He quit drinking and stuck to that too. Having a spare bedroom at my Florida home, I invited him there with me and he didn't hesitate. I explained he would have to adhere to everything I told him to do health-wise, kind of like wellness boot camp and he happily agreed.

Our drive from Massachusetts to Florida was uneventful, except that I had misjudged his ability to navigate feelings. While his cognitive intelligence was mildly impaired, I was amazed at how his brain had recovered since the last time I saw him. His emotional intelligence was actually better than I had ever witnessed. He had a depth of insight that amazed me. He no longer clung to me like a lost puppy as he had often done six years ago. He had a new resilience and a calm demeanor about our relationship and about everything. His attitude was like that of an observer; however the relationship turned out, he seemed at peace with that. This wasn't to be confused with his not caring, because he made it clear that he cared a lot about me, loved me even, but he just insisted he wasn't going to act like an idiot over it, which truthfully he had at times in the past. The heaviness of some dark spiritual force that had surrounded him when I encountered him again in November 2021, had faded and vanished.

Andy stayed in Florida for three weeks with me. We were not intimate; he had his own room, but we spent almost every minute together, romping around the swamps, woods, and beaches of Florida like always. I made sure he ate healthy and exercised daily. By the second week in Florida, his blood pressure was normal. He was still on the antihypertensives, but at least he felt great, looked great, and wasn't having those awful high B/P readings anymore. We were like lovers; except we had no physical relationship. I couldn't do that, not as a true Christian as I felt convicted by the Spirit. Andy said that he understood and that he agreed. In fact, we made a covenant with the Lord. I was having a hard time grasping that there were aspects of him that had changed, matured. When one goes through all that he did, having walked through the fire, one simply can't come out on the other side of that trauma in the same condition as one went in. Andy left Florida in the best of shape. Once home, he continued eating right and maintained his good health.

But, before he left, in fact just an hour before I brought Andy to the airport, he got down on one knee and proposed to me. Slightly put off, yet not surprised, I paused; The Spirit whispered, "This is the one who gave everything he had for you, just as our Lord gave everything. This man would also give it all away for our Lord." Having humbled himself, emptied himself, and come to the end of himself, I instantly saw how much I could learn from him! Not knowing at one time just how this would all turn out; I did know now; Andy's hard path was finally over. His arduous transformation, his newly-won equanimity as he has grown into our Father's arms; this was his glory. "Behold, I am doing a new thing; now it springs forth, do you not perceive it? I will make a way in the wilderness and rivers in the desert" (Isa. 43:19 ESV).

I said yes.

Chapter 23

Personal Pentecost ~ The Real Magic

I HAVE LIVED IN FLORIDA during winter, sometimes in the lush swamps of Ona, Florida, among the alligators and Anhinga with no phone, Wi-Fi, or electricity. I had done this yearly for some time, and there, I am able to be still, know God, and have peace. I take copious nature photos and capture the essence of the animal spirits whom I encounter. These are God's creations, on loan to me while I am living among them. It was here, in 2020, that I had my own personal Pentecost.

All our Pentecost's are personal, but for me, I had the specific intention of sitting with the Holy Spirit and getting to know Him better. There is no place like nature for me to do this. I also wanted to reflect more on Red Dragon, and what I should do with his message and story. Out in the swamp,

I found a little dragonfly pool, with half a dozen different species of dragonflies. There, among them, the largest and prettiest, was an orange-red dragonfly, bigger than my "Red" back north, and every bit as lovely. He was the only dragonfly to stay still so I could photograph him. All the others were skittish and flew away before I could capture them with camera. This "Red" waited until I was done photographing him. I took that as one message to tell my story because the red dragonfly persists, and so should this story. During that time, upon my return from Florida, several people also reiterated that the world needed to hear my story and its message. I just waited on God.

Giving of ourselves is the pathway to the Divine. When we cast our burden upon Christ, we go free. Not totally free, however, we owe our life. Active faith is the bridge over which I pass to the promised land. We are all powerful creators in The Lord. Without His power, we cannot live in the way we are purposed. We were not given a spirit of fear, but rather a spirit of love that gains strength from an underlying, yet almighty, eternal God that knows no limitation, no weakness, and no fear.

"The initial situation of a complex system cannot be accurately determined, so, the future of that complex system cannot be accurately predicted." (Heisenberg Uncertainty Principle.) But we place our faith and trust in God, where there is always a just and predictable outcome. With the Holy Spirit, there is no order in the difficulty of guidance; He leads all of us, regardless of our histories. Just know that human control is an illusion.

Real magic is the art of bringing gifts from another world into this one, and with a foot in two worlds, I'm well-positioned to join those worlds together and include all the worlds in-between with all their timeless frequencies. Behold the grace of God in the intricacies of nature. Experience the grace of God as the Holy Spirit Who guides us in right ways. Visualize in dreams how the Spirit is guiding us. The grace of God is our assurance that we are never alone. I give thanks for this Divine gift and blessing of God's love in my life with the ability to pass it on. Remember, "service to others is the rent we pay for our room here on earth" (Muhammad Ali).

The Affinity House flourishes, while we work closely with the Anchor of Hull, which adds to a strong community-driven recovery base, and Bloom Where You're Planted is busier than ever. I am amazed at its success. Andy will be helping me with the physical part of this business, which is most of it! It'll give us a place in nature to prosper while we beautify their homes and gardens, making them happy. I never thought I would like living surrounded by people, but these are not just people. These are ten women committed to and working on their recovery. Women just like me, except they are at the beginning of their recovery journey. Their ages range from 25-up. We are alike in our addiction and alcoholism. My true belonging is with God, His Holy Spirit, with Jesus, and His living Word. Wherever He plants me, I look to Him to bloom. I can't do anything without him; he lights up my world. In his quiet way, Andy does too. How and when our marriage unfolds remains to be discovered. Who could have imagined?

At first reticent to hear the call to ministry, I welcome it now with an open heart. Who would ever have thought! Fortunately for me, the Nazarenes, like Jesus, are forgiving and accepting, and have allowed me into ministry despite my less-than-holy past. They recognize I am well-positioned to minister to the broken, the disenfranchised, and the outliers on the fringe, having been there myself. I have just acquired my District License in Ministry. I am excited for whatever God-directed adventures await—I am available!

I've given so much thought over time as to why a little red dragonfly, a.k.a., "Red Dragon," would lead me to The Lord. Especially one who I named "Red Dragon" long before I ever read the Bible! I still ponder this. We do assume that God has a sense of humor, because humans perceive and express humor and we are made in God's own image (Gen. 1:27), so doesn't this offer a logical argument for God's humor? The Holy Spirt *is* God, so, while the Lord probably doesn't solicit our reactions with side-splitting wit, no doubt, the Holy Spirit isn't totally above using some irony now and again. Or maybe that name "Red Dragon" had to come to be so that some other message could be delivered for me down the road to validate this whole experience with a brilliance that only God can pull off–this seemed plausible although I couldn't even begin to visualize what God's searing genius would be imparting this knowledge. Then again, maybe I just really don't need to know. God has many why's and how's that remain a great mystery to us. What matters is what becomes of us from the metamorphosis as we repent and are forged through fire, emerging purified and diamond-like, on the other side ~ the side of God.

The Lesson of Red Dragon is clear: "Live a life *of* love, *in* love. Change what you must to live life on fire with passion & creativity for Jesus. Spread His good news and 'show up' in your authenticity, let yourself get 'carried away' on the breezes of His heart's will for you. In so doing, you recommit to your relationship with God. Also, you strengthen your relationship with yourself, your spouse, your tribe, your church, your community, the world, the universe, and the cosmos. Shed the old, be as if new; cleansed & pure; reborn. Pick up your cross and follow in His footsteps! Recreate, repent, and be Who You Truly Are; Christ-like. Be one with The Lord ~ the Holy Spirit, Who loves through you as you spread Faith,

Hope, Joy, and His miraculous blessings to all, to those who long for more, and to all whom you touch, like the kiss of the dragonfly, one being at a time."

A curious thing has happened. While the red dragonfly still flies by me or around me, and still sits awhile with me, his sense of persistence and urgency is gone and he exists now in a quieter place. Could it be that he passed his baton, served his purpose as messenger? He knows Jesus, God, and the Holy Spirit are in me now and he can rest with that. The work of deliverance is done. Red Dragon was not the Holy Spirit, and he wasn't Satan either; he was used by the Holy Spirit to get my attention and then it was the Holy Spirit speaking to me through him. I praise the Lord for such persistence!

I know this remarkable advent has just begun. Our message is to demonstrate that anyone who opens their heart to God, to Jesus, to the Holy Spirit can joyously live life and belong in the Lord's Holy Family with passion, purpose, and joy in servitude. Red–the color of the Pentecost! Our vision is for God's magical, miraculous blessings to encompass all, creating Heaven on Earth, through Jesus Christ our Lord & Savior.

How do I know this?

One little red dragonfly told me so.

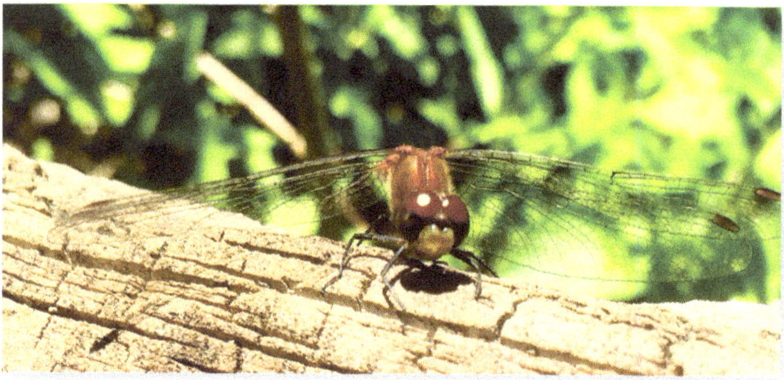

Epilogue

My Love Affair with the Holy Spirit

Jesus promised He would send a helper; He wouldn't leave us orphaned on the planet. "If you love Me, keep My commandments. And I will pray to the Father, and He will give you another Helper, that He may abide with you forever— the Spirit of truth, whom the world cannot receive, because it neither sees Him nor knows Him; but you know Him, for He dwells with you and will be in you. I will not leave you orphans; I will come to you" (John 14: 15-18 NKJV). But the Spirit is elusive... "The wind blows where it chooses, and you hear the sound of it, but you do not know where it comes from or where it goes. So it is with everyone who is born of the Spirit" (John 3:8 NRSV). As esoteric as this all sounds, I fell in love with the Holy Spirit. And once I did, the red dragonfly hung out with me less. I believe this is because now the Spirit does, the Holy Spirit—God's presence here on earth.

I used to believe I would always be a single woman. I am used to this, and most of the time I have been fine with it. I have been single most of my life and am pretty self-contained as far as "needing" a human partner. Once in a while, though, in certain instances, I had felt like it would be nice to have someone to do fun things with, as I mention in my text. Prior to knowing Jesus, I doubt I could have gotten married. I was just too selfish. Since Him, my whole perspective has changed. I live to serve the Lord now. Motherhood is a selfless endeavor at times but serving our Lord is a higher octave of this art. On another level, I love Andy, I know he needs my help and I need his; I'm happy to serve. I sure never saw this coming.

These are all common happenings for me now: Providing service and admitting I need help; walking with the Lord and embracing the wisdom of the Spirit. Yes, the Spirit; so transcendent, divine, aerial, and airy, entrancing, and heavenly. My love of birds and all who fly somehow resounds with the Holy Spirit and reflects the Spirit's true essence back at me. An instructor at Bible College had told me often we identify with one member of the Trinity more than the other two. It isn't that we believe in the others any less, but that there is some characteristic or feature of one member that captivates us more than the others, even though they are all God. For me, the Holy Spirit is my heavenly counterpart. I am just an earthen vessel, but when full of the Spirit, I am so much more. I am more Christlike, more God-like, even though I am only a lowly human. The Spirit lifts me up, gives me the gift of prophesy and occasionally shows me the supernatural. He makes me such a more lovely version of myself. Was this what I experienced as a little child throughout my first years?

There were things that happened to me as a kid that I couldn't explain then and can't to this day. For example, seeing a toy that was be broken, closing my eyes and feeling profound grief over it, and oddly opening my eyes to see the toy was fixed when only a couple moments had gone by. How'd that happen? I ran and told my mother and she told me I was dreaming because "those things don't just happen." Then she'd laugh and say, "oh, you and your dreams!" I remember seeing blacker-than-black entities that looked like someone had cut a weirdly almost-human form out of the fabric of the landscape, showing through a flat, black figure that moved faster than light and yet, in the night it was so much darker than night and it was afraid of ME! What was *that*? So many mysteries! Did the Holy Spirit give me the power of sight to see these things, to experience them? There are so many more, I can't tell them all here, but suffice it to say, these are mysteries to me still to this day, just like the Spirit and the Holy Trinity is a mystery.

When I think back on my life with all its risks, ridiculously bad choices, almost unspeakable trauma, and horrifyingly self-destructive twists and turns, I have to believe in that miracle known as prevenient grace–that divine grace that precedes human decision. God started showing His love to me in my lifetime before I ever knew Him, yet He knew me. I am realizing it was a lot earlier than I ever would have imagined, like before I was born, which tells me I had to have worked awfully hard to resist Him for so many years. I am amazed He kept trying to reach me. It is no wonder that He sent Red Dragon to shock me out of my foolish idiocy of a life and draw me down the shimmering, scintillating, gossamer path of the Spirit.

I wouldn't have thought that with all the people in the world needing faith, that He would have persisted for so long in finding me. He is a God that seeks. This fact alone tells me He has something important for me to do. I have thrown my stake into the ground and said, "Yes, I'm in! I'm available." I am full-on committed to doing the Lord's will and the Kingdom's work as I daily turn my life over to Him. I just humbly await the next chapter. There most certainly is one.

Speaking of God's will, for over seven years, with this story unfolding, formulating, in the works, I always called it the "Lesson Of Red Dragon." I questioned why all the time. I mean, Red Dragon was my red dragonfly, but where did the "lesson" part come from? This title was just always there, long before the story was barely formed; long before I knew or understood anything, including God. I probably named it in its first iterations before I'd written an eighth of it. I just knew it was to be called "Lesson Of Red Dragon," and that there was some lesson, but I had no idea what it was. I left the questions about this "lesson" in the text so you could see the unfolding of this whole incredible message and process, even though, as I write this, the Lord has given me the lesson for which I had prayed on for so many months. In fact, I guess I could've called it the "Message" of Red Dragon, but that never even occurred to me. It would be and always was and still is the "Lesson." As I ended my story, I still was asking, "what *is* the lesson?"

So, what *is* the lesson? Who *is* Red Dragon? How could I publish a story called the "lesson" when I really didn't even know what the full lesson was? Yes, I came to know Christ, that's a very hefty lesson. Still, I wracked my brain not for just a few months, but for several years until I came to believe that Red was a catalyst for the Holy Spirit; uncontrollable, like the wind. But some affirmation that this tiny jewel-red emissary from beyond was a credible messenger from God would be nice, and in fact, it was necessary. This took on the

Spirit's Gift of the "discerning of spirits" that 1 John 4:1-6 speaks of; "We are from God, and whoever knows God listens to us; but whoever is not from God does not listen to us. *This is how we recognize the Spirit of truth and the spirit of falsehood*" (1 John 4:6 NIV). In my story, I make an attempt to "test the spirit of Red Dragon," but I didn't quite know how. Now I was faced with the problem of, "should I publish this?" Did this really, truly come from God, is it *His*? Did The Spirit of God want this story told? Would this story glorify God? How would I know?

I prayed to God on it, asking Him to send me a message, some affirmation that this story should be told and that it was from Him and would glorify Him. Spreading God's Holy Word, His Holy Spirit, and reaching people who were like me; "spiritual" but more in a sensual, New Age way was my goal. Reaching people who desperately needed God but were "on the fence," and didn't know they needed Him was my understanding of my mission. I wasn't telling my story for self-aggrandizement or to make money. No, I would only release it out into the world if it promoted God, Jesus, the Holy Spirit, His Kingdom, God's Holy Word, love, and peace-of-heart, mind, body, and spirit. I could only tell it if it spoke to those people who were seeking but not finding; those who knew something was missing from their lives but didn't immediately recognize that "God-shaped void" in their hearts. If I could know this—I would be humbly grateful. So, I asked God to send me a message or a sign that this story was *of* Him and that He wanted it to be put "out there."

I prayed on it for well over a year with no response, but I continued to pray anyway, remembering Daniel's tenacity in prayer while awaiting God's word. While Archangel Gabriel didn't show up for me, something else almost as great actually did. It came in the form of an awe-inspiring message that literally spelled out the lesson and I nearly fell over on my face. I was "blown away" by the Holy Spirit. I had been contemplating my love for the Holy Spirit, how we abide together, how He has shown me so many things, and opened up my heart and my world. I started to make a note to myself to write about "my love affair with the Holy Spirit" and abbreviated my note, "RDM Holy Spirit" to remind myself to write about it. I paused because even though I knew what I meant, RDM was the acronym for my past business, Red Dragon Magic, so I used it often. Oh well, ok, I told myself, I should probably stop that and start using the acronym for Lesson Of Red Dragon instead. It's about time!

Apparently, I'd not thought about or used the acronym for Lesson Of Red Dragon. So, I thought in my head, ok, L-O-R-D.

Whoa. Wait! Whaaa!?!? That's "Lord!" I instinctively already knew the full meaning. Lesson Of Red Dragon, as an acronym, spells LORD! "When God spoke, it was often unique to the individual," like Moses and the burning bush. And when God spoke, the person knew it was God, again, like Moses did (Blackaby 135). I had no doubt this was a message from God.

"The one who enters by the gate is the shepherd of the sheep. The gatekeeper opens the gate for him, and the sheep listen to his voice. He calls his own sheep by name and leads them out. When he has brought out all his own, he goes on ahead of them, and his sheep follow him because they know his voice" (John 10:2-4 NIV). This was clearly His voice.

This literally "spelled" the affirmation out for me, the lesson *is* the Lord! Jesus, God, the Holy Spirit, heaven, and the Kingdom and so much more. How did I not see this for so long!?!? Ah, yes. Planet for slow learners. This was the affirmation I had prayed for, and I automatically recognized God's "voice!" This is just one of the ways in which we experience God. The Spirit–at work again! He always is. "He has made everything beautiful in its time. He has also set eternity in the human heart; yet no one can fathom what God has done from beginning to end" (Eccles. 3:11 NIV). I love God's mysteries. Even more, I love His revelations.

But mostly, I love Him!!!

See why I am so in love with Him? I was blind but now I see. And *this* was the verification from the Lord that I had been praying on and waiting for. This story needs to be told, that it is of God, *for* God, *for* everyone who needs God's love in their life. And I will be careful to give God all the praise, honor, and glory!

GOD IS LOVE.

How do I know? The Holy Spirit tells me so.

Endnotes

[1] Alexa R, "Witches in History and Legend: Pythia, the Mistress of Divination and Necromancy," Owlcation, April 24, 2020, https://owlcation.com/humanities/Witches-in-History-and-Legend-Pythia-The-Mistress-of-Divination-and-Necromancy.

[2] George B. Murray, MD, "Limbic Music," Journal of Psychosomatics (Volume 33, Issue 1, 1992), 16-23, https://www.sciencedirect.com/science/article/pii/S0033318292720167.

[3] "The Japanese Calendar," National Diet Library, Japan, 2016, https://www.ndl.go.jp/koyomi/e/history/index.html.

> Japanese calendar history: The lunisolar Chinese calendar was introduced to Japan via Korea in the middle of the sixth century. After that, Japan calculated its calendar using

various Chinese calendar procedures, and from 1685, using Japanese variations of the Chinese procedures. In 1873, as part of Japan's Meiji period modernization, a calendar based on the solar Gregorian calendar was introduced.

4   Sarah Zielinski, "14 Fun Facts About Dragonflies," Smithsonian Magazine, October 5, 2011, https://www.smithsonianmag.com/science-nature/14-fun-facts-about-dragonflies-96882693/.

See also: Oregon State University, "Tale of the headless dragonfly: Ancient struggle, preserved in amber," ScienceDaily, October 27, 2010, www.sciencedaily.com/releases/2010/10/101026161257.htm.

5   Sam Ellis, "What Does A Dragonfly Symbolize In The Bible?" Catholics & Bible, November 10, 2020, https://catholicsbible.com/what-does-a-dragonfly-symbolize-in-the-bible/.

6   Ralph D. Lorenze, et al, "Dragonfly: A Rotorcraft Lander Concept for Scientific Exploration," Johns Hopkins APL Technical Digest (Volume 34, Number 3, 2018), www.jhuapl.edu/techdigest, https://dragonfly.jhuapl.edu/News-and-Resources/docs/34_03-Lorenz.pdf.

[7] Dastur Firoze M. Kotwal, "A Brief History of the Parsi Priesthood," Indo-Iranian Journal (Brill, Volume 33, Number 3, July 1990), 165-175, https://www.jstor.org/stable/24655249?refreqid=excelsior%3Afd9031977d70f5c2b4fc00d5a8a1e9f5.

[8] Doris Stickney, *Water Bugs and Dragonflies: Explaining Death to Young Children* (Cleveland: The Pilgrim Press, 1997) pp. 1-16..

[9] Excerpt from the Athanasian Creed, from The Christian Reformed Church: https://www.crcna.org/welcome/beliefs/creeds/athanasian-creed

[10] Frederik van Eeden, "A Study of Dreams," The Lucidity Institute, Proceedings of the Society of Research (Volume 26, 1913), Archived from the original on October 8, 2019, http://www.lucidity.com/vanEeden.html.

> A lucid dream is a type of dream where the dreamer becomes aware that they are dreaming. During a lucid dream, the dreamer may gain some amount of control over the dream characters, narrative, or environment; however, this is not actually necessary for a dream to be described as lucid.

[11] Richard Rohr, *Adam's Return: The Five Promises of Male Initiation*, (New York: The Crossroad Publishing Company, 2004), 135-139.

[12] Hedgewitch: The name Hedgewitch refers to the old, wise women who often lived on the outskirts of town, "beyond the hedge." Today, Appalachia is still rich in folk magic and witchery. For more info, see Beth Rae's "Hedge Witch: A Guide to Solitary Witchcraft," Robert Hale Ltd; New edition, 1992.

[13] Dwight Longenecker, "Miracles and Magic: What's the Difference?" The Stream, July 20, 2019, https://stream.org/miracles-and-magic-whats-the-difference/.

[14] C.L.R. James, *The Black Jacobins: Toussaint L'Ouverture and the San Domingo Revolution*, 2nd edition. (New York: Random House, 1989).

[15] "Thaumaturgy," *Merriam-Webster.com Dictionary*, accessed July 2019 from: Merriam-Webster, https://www.merriam-webster.com/dictionary/thaumaturgy,

[16] Colleen de Bellefonds, "What's a Twin Flame, and How Do You Know If You Found Yours?" Healthline, July 7, 2021, Medically reviewed by Janet Brito, Ph.D., LCSW, CST, https://www.healthline.com/health/mind-body/twin-flame#vs-soulmate.

[17] Adapted from Watchman Nee, *The Normal Christian Life*, Reprinted edition (Carol Stream: Tyndale House Publishers, November 4, 1977), 184-185.

[18] Bernadette King, "Dragon Spirit Guide," What Is My Spirit Animal.com, accessed 2020 from: https://whatismyspiritanimal.com/fantasy-mythical-creatures/dragon-symbolism-meaning/.

[19] Red Dragon Organics, "Myth of the Dragon," http://reddragonorganics.com.au/myth-of-the-dragon.

[20] "Why the Dragonfly?" Dragonfly Transitions, 2002, accessed October 2018 from https://dragonflytransitions.com/why-the-dragonfly/.

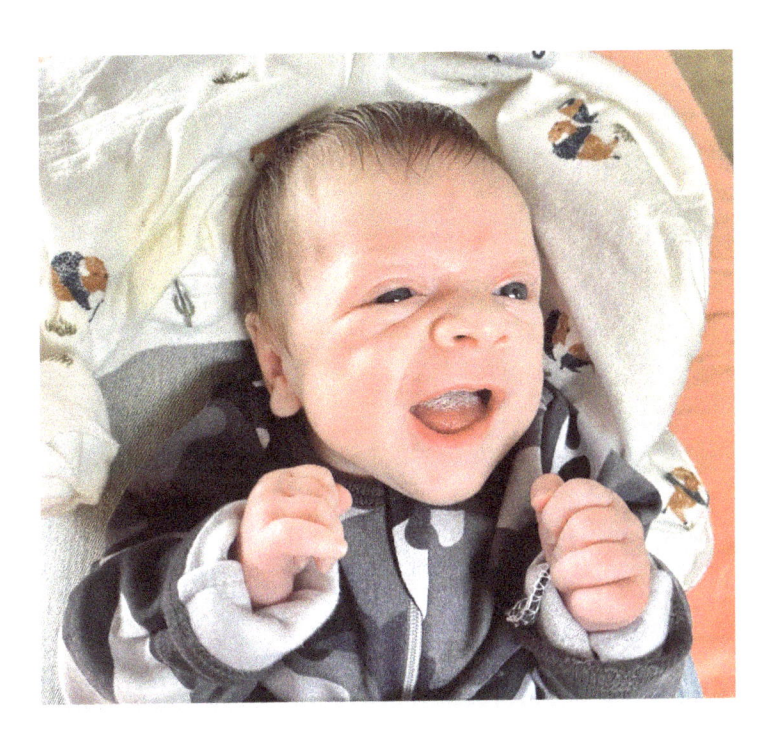

Carter Malachi Heroux was born on 17 September 2022.

Ingram Content Group UK Ltd.
Milton Keynes UK
UKHW021116030423
419480UK00010B/173